THE RIDICULOUSLY SIMPLE GUIDE TO IPHONE X, XR, XS, AND XS MAX

A PRACTICAL GUIDE TO GETTING STARTED WITH THE NEXT GENERATION OF IPHONE AND IOS 12

BRIAN NORMAN

Ridiculously Simple Press
ANAHEIM, CALIFORNIA

Copyright © 2018 by Scott La Counte.

All rights reserved. No part of this publication may be reproduced, distributed or transmitted in any form or by any means, including photocopying, recording, or other electronic or mechanical methods, without the prior written permission of the publisher, except in the case of brief quotations embodied in critical reviews and certain other noncommercial uses permitted by copyright law.

Contents

Introduction 1
Um...So Where Is the Home Button (and Other Changes You Need to Know) 3
    Let's Get Cosmetic, Shall We? 3
    Let's Talk About Your Face 7
    Feature This… 9
    Thanks for the Nice Gesture, Apple! 10
    The Ridiculously Simple Chapter One Recap 18

Hello, World 20
    Setting Things Up 20
    Face ID 22
    I Feel Charged! 30
    How Do You Send Cute Emoji's to Everyone? 33

Just the Basics…and Keep It Simple! 41
    Welcome Home 41
    Making Calls 42
    There's An App for That 45
    Organizing Apps 45
    Messaging 48
    Notifications 57
    Using AirDrop 58

Just the Basics…and Keep It Simple! 60
    Phone 61
    Mail 66
    Surfing the Internet with Safari 67
    iTunes 78
    Apple Music 79
    Buying Apps 79
    Calendar 84
    Weather 86
    Maps 88
    iBooks 92

Health 94
Find My Friends 98
Find iPhone 99
Home 99
ARKit 100

Make It Yours *102*
Screen Time 103
Do Not Disturb Mode 104
General Settings 106
Sounds 108
Privacy 110
Mail, Contacts, Calendars Settings 110
Adding Facebook and Twitter 111
Family Sharing 114

Lights, Camera, Action *116*
Taking Photos and Vidoes 116
Photo Editing 120
Editing Live Photos 122
Photo Albums and Photo Sharing 124

Animoji *127*
How to Add Your Own Animoji 127

Hey, Siri *131*

Maintain and Protect *135*
Security 135
Encryption 136
Keychain 137
iCloud 138
Battery Tips 139

Must-Have Apps *143*

Disclaimer*: this book is not endorsed by Apple, Inc. and should be considered unofficial.*

Introduction

Getting a new iPhone is exciting; it can almost feel like getting a new toy. Nobody likes a toy that makes you read a lengthy manual just to figure out how the darn thing works!

If you've already had an iPhone (or maybe several), then chances are you already know how it works. But the iPhone X will throw you a curveball because the Home button has been removed. I'll help make sure you know how to use the shortcuts and gestures that go along with this transition. It will, of course, also cover all the new features added into iOS 12.

This guide is formatted in a way to help you use your phone (and all it's powerful features) as quickly as possible.

I purposely have written this guide to be a little more casual and fun then what you expect from most iPhone manuals. The iPhone is a fun gadget, and any guide you read should be an equally fun read.

Each chapter starts with bullet points on what will be covered, so if something you already know, you can skip right ahead; if you only need to know how to use new features, the book is also formatted in a way that these stand out.

Are you ready to start enjoying your new iPhone? Then let's get started!

[1]
UM...SO WHERE IS THE HOME BUTTON (AND OTHER CHANGES YOU NEED TO KNOW)

This chapter will cover:
- The iPhones buttons
- What's Face ID
- What are the new features to iOS 12
- How to use the iPhone when it doesn't have a physical Home button

LET'S GET COSMETIC, SHALL WE?

So the real elephant in the room with the iPhone X and up is the Home button or lack thereof. In the next chapter, I'll talk about getting set up, so I know this all sounds a little backwards, but because so many people are upgrading to the new iPhone from an earlier model, it's worth talking about the main things that will be different about it here.

If you have used the iPhone before, then I bet you'll spend a good day continuously putting your thumb where the button used to be! Don't worry! You're going to get through it. In fact, after you get used to it not being there, you'll actually start seeing it's more effective without it.

Before diving into the gestures, let's cover some other things that look different about this phone.

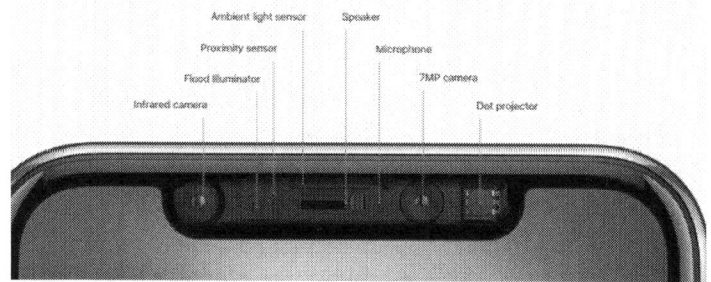

The top portion of the phone (it's known as the top notch) has a lot for there then other phones, doesn't it? All of that helps your phone work better. To the far right is a Dot Projector. It sounds like something that will project your iPhone onto the wall, doesn't it? I wish! That's actually the camera that scans your face for Face ID (I'll cover that in just a second). Next to that is the camera; it's 7MP, which isn't as good as the 12MP camera on the back, but it's certainly an improvement from what was on earlier phones. There's a few other sensors and cameras to the far left. They all sound fancy, don't they? Proximity sensor. Flood illuminator. Fancy is...well fancy! But what on Earth does that mean in simple terms? It means that the front-facing camera can take pretty impressive selfies! If you've used the iPhone 8 or 8+ then you're probably familiar with Portrait mode? If not, in a nutshell, it gives a blurred, professional look to your photo. To do that, you need some extra sensors; the iPhone X and XS have those features and both the front and back of the camera. That means you can get the same quality photos no matter what you use (front or back camera).

Okay, so all that's interesting, right? But you don't actually do anything with the notch. What about the buttons on the phone itself. Good question! Thanks for asking!

The button placement isn't too far off from previous iPhone's.

On the right side, you have your volume up and down, which does, you guessed it! Turns your volume up and down! There's also the switch above it that will silence sound.

On the left side you have your "Side Button." Legend has it, they named it the Side Button because it's on the side of the phone! That button is on other phones--albeit a tad shorter--but it functions a little bit different here.

The Side Button is and isn't the Home button replacement. That sounds vague, huh? Here's what I mean: you won't use this button to get back to the home screen, but you can use it to activate Siri (or you can just say "Hey Siri"). You also use this button to power the phone on and off--or to put it in standby (which is the mode you put it in after you finish playing Angry Birds in the bathroom and need to set the phone down for a minute to wash your hands).

The most common use for the Side Button is to wake up your phone. Picking up your phone and staring at it with an annoyed or confused expression will also do this. But if you ever find yourself stuck and picking up the phone isn't waking it up, then just push down on the Side Button and you should be just fine.

That side button is also going to come in handy when you want to use Apple Pay--double push the button and then stare at your phone sadly as money is magically taken away.

LET'S TALK ABOUT YOUR FACE

Things were going okay with you and the Home button. You could rub your thumb over it and like a genie in a bottle, it would magically read your DNA and turn on. Why'd Apple have to go an ruin a good thing?

Sure getting rid of the button gives you more screen real estate, but plenty of other phones have added a button to the back of the phone so you can have the both of both worlds. It's like Apple is trying to force you to love it, isn't it? I don't know why Apple does everything, but if past history teaches us anything, we have learned that Apple makes us adopt to better things by taking away the things we love. We loved our CD drives...and Apple took them out and put USB drives in their place; we got through it though didn't we?! They did it again with the headphone jack. And on new Macbook's, USB is gone and in its place the faster USB-C.

Change is never fun, but it's not necessarily a bad thing. If you like numbers, you'll love this one. That little finger scanner has a ratio of 50,000:1--that's the ratio of how hard it would be for someone to break into your phone. The iPhone with Face ID? 1,000,000:1. So if you're a phone of security, then Face ID is a no brainer.

If your that person who is always throwing "What if" into the equation (you're the same person who morbidly asked, what if someone stole my phone and cut off my finger to unlock it? Would the fingerprint scanner still work?), then I'm sure you have a few questions. Like:

- What if I wear glasses and then take them off or put in contacts?
- What if I have a beard and shave it?
- What if I think I look like Brad Pitt but the phone says I'm more of a Lyle Lovett?

Sorry, Lyle, not everyone can be a Brad--but you don't have to worry about those first two points. Face ID has adaptive recognition, so you'll be just fine if you decide to grow it out for Movember.

If you're in a dark room, Face ID will also still work--albeit with a little bit of help from the light sensor--which is a little annoying if your lying in bed and the only way to unlock your phone is to have a light turn on to scan your face. If you're in a dark room, you can also just press that side button to open it manually and skip Face ID.

FEATURE THIS...

Every year, Apple dazzles us with dozens of new features. A lot of these features are under the hood, and don't sound very exciting, but they are making your phone perform better. Briefly, here are a few things people are excited about. I'll cover where to find these (and more) as I walk you around the iPhone and show you where things are.

- Facetime with multiple people (up to 32 to be exact); this is basically Apple's way to combat Google Hangouts and Skype. Unfortunately, the feature is coming later in the Fall.
- Animoji - This cute app lets you animate yourself; it was introduced with the iPhone X, but updated for the newest iOS.
- Add stickers and filters when you are on FaceTime or when you take a picture in iMessage.
- Screen time - The greatest and most depressing feature of the new iOS! This app tells us exactly how long we're using our phones.
- Control your Notifications - With the newest iOS, notifications are grouped together (so if you have 40 emails and 10 text, it will show only one and when you press it, you can see what's stacked under it); you can also control how notifications are delivered--if you want them sent quietly, for example (you get the notification in Notification Center, but not on the lock screen--and it's delivered without a chime).
- Share more than photos - previously, you could share photos; in the new iOS you can share memories--so if you have a group of photos from that amazing trip to Boring Town, USA, you can share them with all of your friends.
- If you want the big giant list of everything new in iOS 12, visit: https://www.apple.com/ios/ios-12/features/

THANKS FOR THE NICE GESTURE, APPLE!

And now the moment you've been reading for: how to make your way around a phone without the button.

Let's Go Home

First, the easiest gesture: getting to your Home screen. Do you have your pen and paper ready? It's complicated....swipe up from the bottom of your screen. That's it.

It's not too far off from pushing a button. Heck, your fingers even in the same place! The only difference is your moving your thumb upward instead of inward.

Multitask

As Dorothy would say, there's no place like Home--but we can still give a shoutout to multitask can't we? If you don't know what it is, Multitask is how you switch quickly between apps--you're in iMessage and want to open up Safari to get a website, for example; instead of closing iMessage, finding Safari from the Home screen, and then repeating the process to get back, you use multitask to do it quickly.

On the old iPhone's you would double press the Home button. On the new iPhone, you Swipe Up from the bottom as if you were going to home...but don't lift your finger; instead of lifting your finger, continue swiping up until you reach the middle of your screen--at this point, you should see the multitask interface.

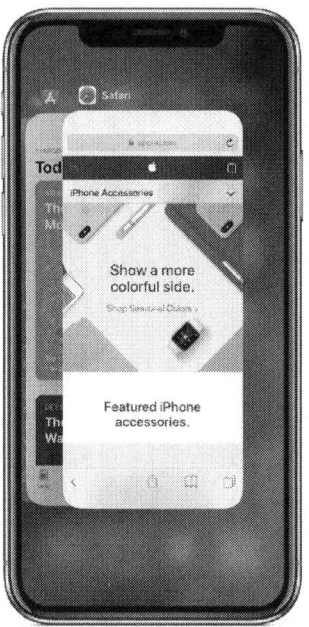

If you have an app open (Note: this does not work on the Home screen), you can also slide your finger right across the bottom edge of the screen; this will go to the previous app open.

Mission Control...We're Go for Flashlight

If you haven't noticed, I'm putting these features in other of use. So the third most common gesture people use is the Control Center. That's where all your Controls are located--go figure...Control is where controls are!

We'll go over Control panel closer later in the book. For now, just know that this where you'll do things like adjust brightness, enable airplane mode, and turn on the beloved flashlight. On the old iPhone, you accessed Control Center by swiping up from the bottom of the screen. No Bueno on the new iPhone--if you recall, swiping up gets you Home.

To new gesture for Control Center is swiping down from the upper right corner of the iPhone (not the top middle, which will do something else).

Notify Me How to Get Notifications

Eck! So many gestures to remember! Let me throw you a bone. To see notifications (those are the alerts like email and text that you get on your phone), swipe down from the middle of the screen. That's the same way you did it before! Finally, nothing new to remember!

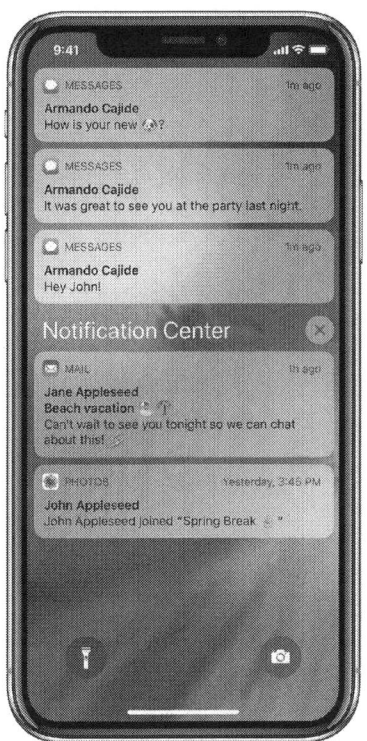

I hate to steal your bone back, but about not remembering anything: there is something to remember. :-(

12 | *The Ridiculously Simple Guide to iPhone X*

If you swipe down from the right corner you get the Control Center; that wasn't the case on old phones. Swiping down anywhere on top got you to the home screen. On the X and up, you can only swipe in the middle.

Searching for Answers

If you're like me, you probably have a million apps--and because you want to see the wallpaper on your phone's Home screen, you put those million apps in one folder! That may not be the best way to organize a library, but the search function on the iPhone, makes it easy to find anything quickly.

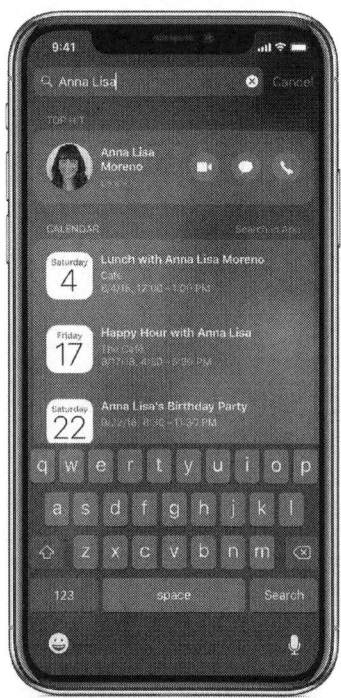

In addition to apps, you can use search to find calendar dates, contacts, things on the Internet. The best part of search? Works the same way it does on older iPhones...there's your bone back! From your Home screen, swipe down in the middle of the screen.

Calling All Widgets

Many apps come with what's known as a Widget. Widgets are basically mini versions of your favorite app--so you can see the weather, for example, without actually opening the app.

The gesture to see widgets is the same on the new phone as the old. Hurray! Something else you don't have to learn. From the Home or Lock screen, swipe right and they'll come out.

Reach for the Sky

Several years ago, Apple made a big change to the iPhone by making things...well big! They introduced what would be known as the "plus" model. It was wonderful...and big! If you had Shaq hands, then you'd have no problem getting around the device. If you had normal human hands, then the apps on the top row of the phone were a bit of a stretch to reach with one hand.

This wasn't a huge problem on the iPhone X because it was a little smaller than the plus. The next generation phones, however, introduced a "max" model. On the old phones, this was a snap--just double tap (not press, tap) the Home button. New phones? Sorry, but we're back to learning new things...I'm all out of bones for this chapter.

To reach the top, swipe down on the bottom edge of the screen.

THE RIDICULOUSLY SIMPLE CHAPTER ONE RECAP

Okay, so you only got a minute to get up and running, and you need the 1 minute summary of everything important?

Let's cover gestures. The right side will be the way the gesture used to work, and left side will be the way it works on new iPhones.

iPhone 8 and Down	iPhone X and Up
Go to the Home screen - Press the Home button.	Go to the Home screen - Swipe up from the bottom of your screen.
Multitask - Double press Home button.	Multitask - Swipe up from the bottom of your screen, but don't lift your finger until it reaches the middle of the screen.
Control Center - Swipe up from the bottom of the screen.	Control Center - Swipe down from the upper right corner of the iPhone.
Notifications - Swipe down from the top of the screen.	Notifications - Swipe down from the middle top of the screen.
Search - From the Home screen, swipe down from the middle of your screen.	Search - From the Home screen, swipe down from the middle of your screen.
Access Widgets - From the Home or Lock screen, swipe right.	Access Widgets - From the Home or Lock screen, swipe right.
Reach the Top - Double tap (not press) the home	Reach the Top - Swipe down on the bottom edge

| button. | of the screen. |

[2]
Hello, World

This chapter will cover:
- Setting up your iPhone for the first time
- Setting up your iPhone with your previous phones settings
- Setting up Face ID
- Charging
- Navigating around the phone using gestures, 3D touch and more
- Using the on-screen keyboard

SETTING THINGS UP

Now that you know about the main differences between the physical nature of the phone, let's take a set back and talk about setting it up. If you're already at the Home screen, you can obviously skip this section.

Unboxing the iPhone shouldn't throw you any curveballs. It doesn't have a manual, but that's normal for Apple. You can find the manual on Apple's website (https://support.apple.com/manuals/iphone) if that's something you'd like to see. It's also free on iBooks. What is worth pointing out is the headphones. A few years back, Apple decided for us that we no longer needed a normal headphone jack. How sweet, right? But to be nice, they always threw in a 3.5m Lighting Adaptor--so you could use any headphones when it was plugged in. This year's model ditches that. If you're keen on using it, then you can buy one for under $10.

Once you turn the phone on with the side button, it will load to a setup screen. Setup can be intimating to a lot of people, but Apple's setup is probably the easiest one you'll ever do--even my mom, who hates all electronics, had no problem doing it on her own.

It's pretty straightforward. I suppose I could just write everything that you'll see on the screen, but it seems a little counterproductive since you are seeing it on the screen. In a nutshell, it's going to ask you your preferred language and country, your wireless network (make sure you connect to your wireless network here, or it's going to start downloading a lot of apps over your LTE, which will eat up your data), and you'll need to activate your device with your wireless carrier.

So that's the basics. There's a few options after here that might be a little less straightforward. The first is a question that asks if you want Location Services turned on. I recommend saying yes. This is how the Map will automatically know where you are, or when you take a photo at Boring Town, USA, and several years later you say "where on Earth was this photo taken?" You'll know exactly where it was taken if Location Services is turned on. Remember: anything you don't turn on here (or that you turn on) can be changed later. So if you change your mind, it's fine.

> You Should Know: Anytime Location Services is being used in an app, you will see a small arrow icon in the upper right corner of your screen.

FACE ID

Face ID is probably one of the features you hear about the most. It lets your phone scan your face to unlock it-- it's more secure than your fingerprint. To get started, just tap the get started button.

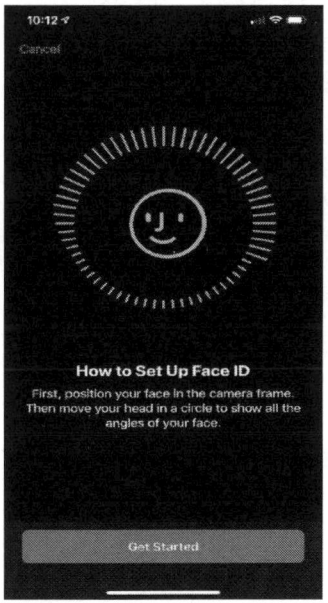

Next you'll be directed to put your face in the center of the camera, and you basically move your head around, so the camera can see all of your features. It's kind of like rolling your next around. It takes about 20 seconds to complete.

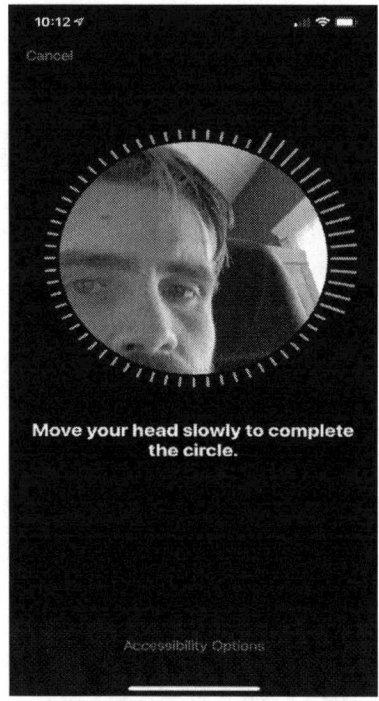

Once it's done, you'll get a message. That's it. Your phone is now ready to unlock at the site of your gorgeous face!

After you set up Face ID, you'll be prompted to enter a passcode. Why do you need a passcode when you have have a Face ID? The biggest reason is there may be times when you don't want to use Face ID (like it's dark and you don't want a bunch of light illuminated from your phone) or you have a friend who needs to get into your phone.

By default, the passcode is six digits. If you don't want to add one, tap "Don't Add Passcode"; in this same area, you can also change it to a four-digit passcode. My only advice here is to be creative: don't use the same four digits as your bank pin, or the last four of your social. And remember: you can change it later.

Once security options are set up, you'll have the option to restore from a backup. If you have a previous iPhone, I would recommend doing this--it will save you time adjusting some of the settings later.

If you have decided to restore from a backup, then make sure your backup is up-to-date. On your old iPhone, go to Settings, then tap your name on the top (it will probably have a picture of you), next tap iCloud, and finally go to iCloud Backup. It might be set to automatic. Just to make sure you get everything, however, I would tap Back Up Now. Below the Back Up Now option, you can see when the last backup was performed.

You're almost done! But first Apple needs to understand how to take your money! The next screen is creating an Apple ID. If you already have one, the sign in; if you don't have one, then create a free one. Don't want to give Apple your hard earned money? I don't blame you! They did, after all, just take $1,000+ from you for your phone! But you still need an Apple ID. Don't worry--you don't have to give them any more money if you really don't want to, but I'm sure you'll want to download Free apps (like Facebook), and you'll need an Apple ID for that as well.

Once your phone is all done thinking about how it will take your money, it will be time to setup iCloud. Again, this is something I recommend setting up. iCloud backs everything up remotely; so if you want to share things across multiple devices (your Apple Watch, iPad, Macbook, Apple TV, for example) it's a breeze.

After iCloud is Apple Pay. "Wait," you say! "I thought Apple already asked how they were going to get more money?!" They did! This is all about how others will take your money! Once you have an expensive phone, everyone wants a piece of you! Apple Pay will basically create a virtual credit card so when you're at the grocery store, you can pay by tapping your phone instead of whipping out your wallet.

Is Apple Pay really safe? In a word: yes. It's safer than the card you carry around in your wallet. Unlike that card, no one can see the numbers on it and if someone were to steal your phone, they wouldn't be able to use Apple Pay unless they knew your password. The encryption on Apple Pay is also much more sophisticated--you are much more likely to get your number hacked online than on your phone.

Most banks are on Apple Pay, but unfortunately, some are not. If you don't see yours, you will have to wait. You can't add it manually.

Next up is iCloud Keychain. Like most things in the setup, it's all about what you are comfortable with. Keychain stores all your passwords in one place. So if you are shopping online, you don't have to add it in or remember it. It's all secure--no one can see it but you. And, of course, you can turn it on or off later.

Only a few more steps! Painless so far, right?

Up next is Siri. Siri is your personal assistant. You can say things like "Hey, Siri: what's the weather" and like magic, she'll tell you. I'll cover it later in the book, but for now I would turn it on.

24 | *The Ridiculously Simple Guide to iPhone X*

After enabling Siri, decide whether or not to report diagnostic and usage data to Apple. If you're worried about privacy, tap the About Diagnostics and Privacy to learn what information Apple will receive and how it will be used.

Finally, decide whether or not you'd like to use a zoomed-in display or not. If you prefer larger icons, you can choose Zoomed View for a magnified display. It's entirely up to you, and this setting can be changed later.

Scott La Counte | 25

And finally, setup is done! The last screen says "Welcome to iPhone - Get Started" tapping on that will bring you to the Home screen, and that's where the fun really starts.

I Feel Charged!

Before digging into using your phone deeper, I want to talk real quick about charging. You probably know how to plug the charger into your phone. If you can't figure out how to stick an out-y into an in-y, then call that nephew who never returns your phone call and ask him. He's going to love hearing from you, I'm sure.

What might not be so obvious is the iPhone doesn't need to be plugged into anything to be charged. new iPhones can be charged wirelessly. To do this you need what's called a "Qi charger." They're not terribly expensive ($20 range). Qi chargers are compatible with other phones, so a lot of cafes and hotels have them ready to use. To use it, you just set it on top of the wireless charging mat and make sure the charging light (⚡) comes on the phone. It's really simple.

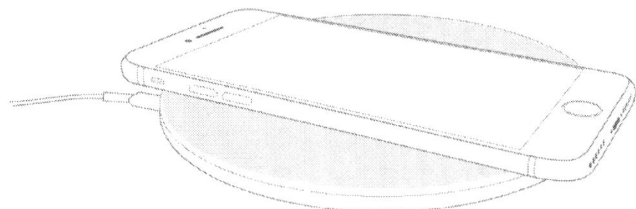

Enough About Setup! How Do I Use This Thing, Already!

The iPhone is a touchscreen device, so to use it you'd think you'd have to worry about only one thing: touching it!

That's true. But there are different ways you can touch it. Fortunately, unlike gestures (mentioned in Chapter One), nothing has really changed; so if you know how to use an iPhone with 3D Touch on previous phones, you'll be just fine. Below is a quick summary:

Tap

This is the "click" of the iPhone world. A tap is just a brief touch. It doesn't have to be hard or last very long. You'll tap icons, hyperlinks, form choices, and more. You'll also tap numbers on a touch keypad in order to make calls. It's not exactly rocket science, is it!

Tap and Hold

This simply means touching the screen and leaving your finger in contact with the glass. It's useful for bringing up context menus or other options in some apps.

Double Tap

This refers to two rapid taps, like double clicking with your finger. Double tapping will perform different functions in different apps. It will also zoom in on pictures or webpages.

3D Touch: Press

So here's where it gets a little tricky--but it's really not that complicated. 3D Touch is basically how hard you press down. If you press the glass screen as though you were pressing a button, you can "peek" into items like Mail messages, previewing them without fully opening them. Then just press a little harder to "pop" the message open.

Swipe

Swiping means putting your finger on the surface of your screen and dragging it to a certain point and then removing your finger from the surface. You'll use this motion to navigate through menu levels in your apps, through pages in Safari, and more. It'll become second nature overnight, I promise.

Drag

This is mechanically the same as swiping, but with a different purpose. You'll touch an object to select it, and then drag it to wherever it needs to go and release it. It's just like dragging and dropping with a mouse, but it skips the middleman.

Pinch

Take two fingers, place them on the iPhone screen, and move them either toward each other or away from each other in a pinching or reverse pinching motion. Moving your fingers together will zoom in inside many apps, including web browsers and photo viewers; moving them apart will zoom out.

Rotate and Tilt

Many apps on iPhone take advantage of rotating and tilting the device itself. For instance, in the paid app Star Walk, you can tilt the screen so that it's pointed at whatever section of the night sky you're interested in – Star Walk will reveal the constellations based on the direction the iPhone is pointed.

How Do You Send Cute Emoji's to Everyone?

The reason you got an iPhone is to send adorable emoji's with your text messages, obviously! So how do you do it! It's all in the keyboard, so I'll cover that next!
Anytime you type a message, the keyboard pops up automatically. There are no extra steps. But there are a

few things you can do with the keyboard to make it more personal.

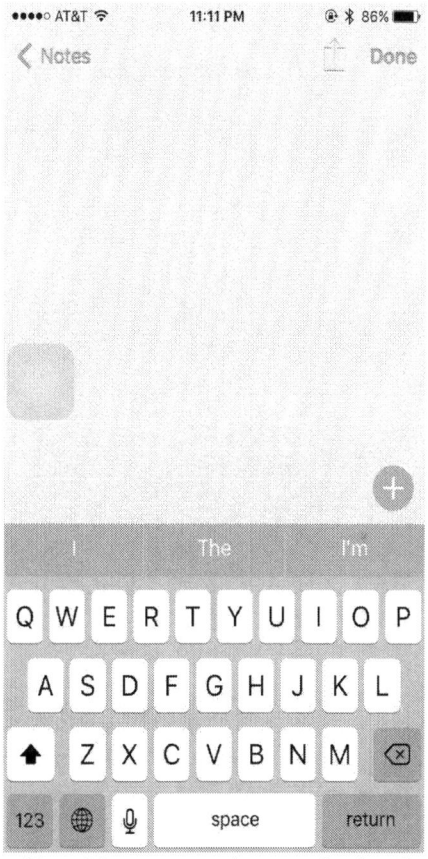

There are a few things to notice on the keyboard – the delete key is marked with a little x (it's right next to the letter M), and the shift key is the key with the upward arrow (next to the letter Z).

By default, the first letter you type will be capitalized. You can tell what case the letters are in though at a quick glance.

To use the shift key, just tap it and then tap the letter you want to capitalize or the alternate punctuation you'd like to use. Alternatively, you can touch the shift key and drag your finger to the letter you want to capitalize.

Double tap the shift key to enter caps lock (i.e. everything is capitalized) and tap once to exit caps lock.

Special Characters

To type special characters, just tap and hold the key of the associated letter until options pop up. Drag your finger to the character you want to use, and be on your way. What exactly would you use this for? Let's say you're are writing something in Spanish and need the accent on the "e"; tapping and holding on the "e" will bring that option up.

Using Dictation

Let's face it: typing on the keyboard stinks sometimes! Wouldn't be easier to just say what you want to write? If that sounds like you, then Dictation can help! Just tap the microphone next to the spacebar and start talking. It works pretty well.

Number and Symbol Keyboards

Of course, there's more to life than letters and exclamation marks. If you need to use numbers, tap the 123 key in the bottom left corner. This will bring up a different keyboard with numbers and punctuation.

From this keyboard, you can get back to the alphabet by tapping the ABC key in the bottom left corner. You can also access an additional keyboard which includes the remaining standard symbols by tapping the #+- key, just above the ABC key.

Emoji Keyboard

And finally, the moment you've waited for! Emoji's!
The emoji keyboard is accessible using the smiley face key between the 123 key and the dictation key. Emojis are tiny cartoon images that you can use to liven

up your text messages or other written output. This goes far beyond the colon-based emoticons of yesteryear - there are enough emojis on your iPhone to create an entire visual vocabulary.

To use the emoji keyboard, note that there are categories along the bottom (and that the globe icon on the far left will return you to the world of language). Within those categories, there are several screens of pictographs to choose from. Many of the human emojis include multicultural variations. Just press and hold them to reveal other options.

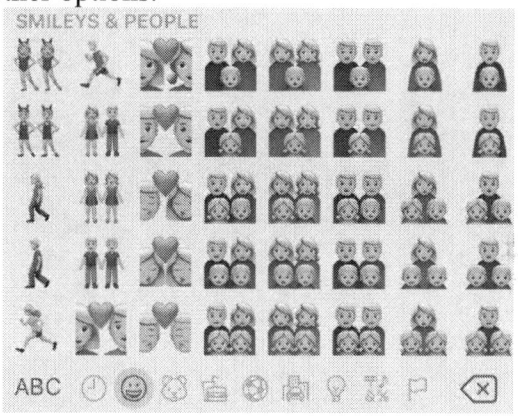

Multilingual Typing

Most people are probably all set. They know all they need to know about typing on the iPhone and they're ready to blast emoji's at their friends. There are a few other features that apply to some (not all people)

One such feature is Multilingual Typing. This is for people who type multiple languages at the same time. So if you type between Spanish and English, you won't keep seeing a message saying your spelling is wrong.

If that sounds like you, then you just need to enable another dictionary, which is simple. Go to Settings > General > Dictionary.

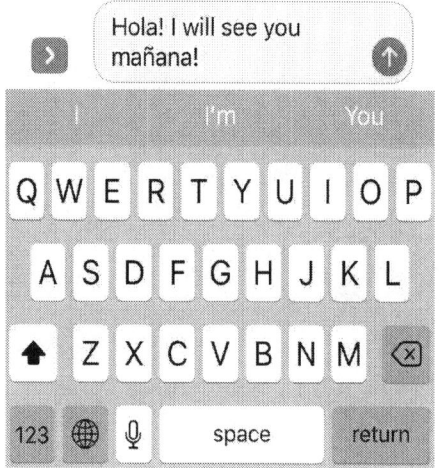

Configuring International Keyboards

If you find yourself typing in a different language fairly often, you may want to set up international keyboards. To set up international keyboards, visit Settings > General > Keyboard > Keyboards. You can then add an appropriate international keyboard by tapping Add New Keyboard. As an example, iPhone has great support for Chinese text entry – choose from pinyin, stroke, zhuyin, and handwriting, where you actually sketch out the character yourself.

When you enable another keyboard, the smiley emoji key will change to a globe icon. To use international keyboards, tap the Globe key to cycle through your keyboard choices.

Your iPhone is loaded with features to help prevent slip-ups, including Apple's battle-tested autocorrect feature, which guards against common typos. In iOS 8, Apple introduced a predictive text feature that predicts what words you're most likely to type, and its accuracy is even better in the new iOS.

Three choices appear just above the keyboard – the entry as typed, plus two best guesses. Predictive text is somewhat context-specific, too. It learns your speech patterns as you email your boss or text your best friend, and it will serve up appropriate suggestions based on who you're messaging or emailing. Of course, if it bothers you, you can turn it off by visiting Settings > General > Keyboards and turning off predictive text by sliding the green slider to the left.

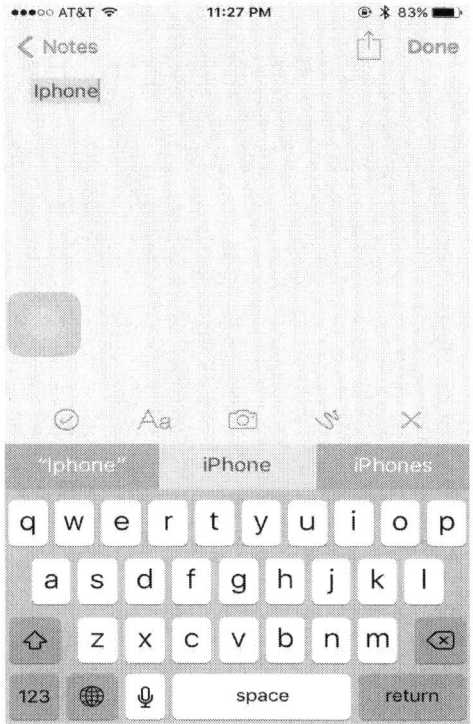

Third Party Keyboards

Lastly, you can add third-party keyboards to your phone. So if you hate the iPhone keyboard and want something similar to what's on Android, then you can go to the App Store and get it (more on that later)

[3]
JUST THE BASICS...AND KEEP IT SIMPLE!

This chapter will cover:
- Home Screen
- Making Calls
- Adding and removing apps
- Sending messages
- iMessage Apps
- Notifications
- AirDrop

WELCOME HOME

There's one thing that has pretty much stayed the same since the very first iPhone was released: the Home screen. The look has evolved, but the layout has not. All you need to know about it is it's the main screen. So when you read me say "go to the Home scree" this is the screen I'm talking about. Make sense?

Making Calls

You know what always amazes me when I see commercials for the iPhone? It's a phone, but people never seem to be talking on it! But it actually can make phone calls!

If you actually need to call someone, then tap the green Phone icon in the lower left corner of your home screen. This will bring up the iPhone's keypad. Tap in your number and hit the green Call button. To hang up, just tap the red End button at the bottom of the screen. You'll see other options on the call screen, too. If you needed to use the keypad while on a call, just tap the Keypad circle to bring it up. Similarly, you can mute a call or put it on speaker here.

Receiving a call is fairly intuitive. When your phone rings, your iPhone will tell you who's calling. If their name is stored in your contacts (more on this later), it'll be displayed. All you have to do is swipe to answer the call. There are some additional options as well – you can ask iPhone to remind you of the call later by tapping Remind Me, or you can respond with a text message. iOS 12 includes some handy canned responses, including "can't talk right now…", "I'll call you later," "I'm on my way", and "What's up?" You can also send a custom message if you need to. If you miss a call, iPhone will let you know the next time you wake up your phone. By default, you can respond to a missed call directly from the lock screen.

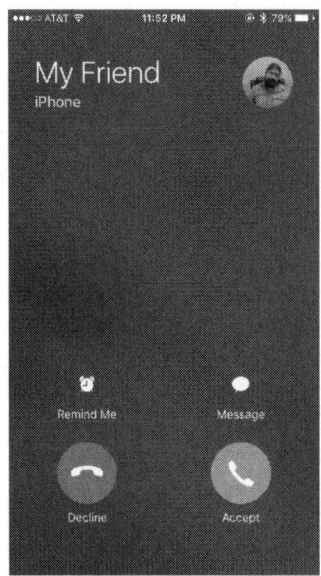

When a call from an unknown number comes in, iPhone will check other apps like Mail where phone numbers might be found. Using that information, it will make a guess for you and let you know who might be calling. Kind of creepy, right? But also really useful.

If you want to feel extra special, you can have Siri announce your call. To turn this feature on, go to Settings > Phone > Announce Calls. Select Always, Headphones & Car, Headphones Only or Never to choose your preferred way to announce calls.

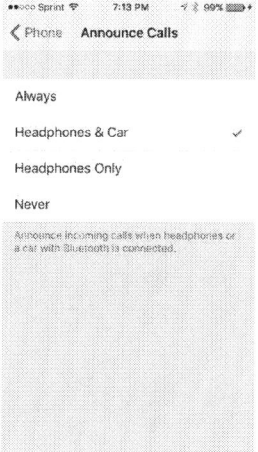

There's An App for That

App is short for application. So when you hear the term "There's an app for that." It just means there's a program that does what you want to do. If you're a Windows use, all those things you always open (like Word and Excel) are apps. Apple has literally millions of apps. Opening an app is as simple as touching it.

Unlike apps on a computer, you don't have to close apps on your phone. It's all automatic. For most apps, it will even remember where you were so when you open it again, it's saved.

Organizing Apps

If you're like me--and pretty much most people are-- you love your apps and you have a lot of them! So you'll need to know how to move them around, put them in folders, and delete them. It's all easy to do.

The Home screen may be the first screen you see, but if you swipe to the right, you'll see there's more; you can have 11. Personally, I keep the most used apps on the first screen, and not so used apps in folders on the second. The bottom dock is where I put the apps I use all the time (like mail and Safari).

To rearrange apps, take your finger and touch one of your apps. Instead of tapping, hold your finger down for a few seconds--don't push too hard, however, or you'll activate the 3D Touch. Notice how all of your apps start jiggling? When the apps are jiggling like that, you can touch them without opening them and drag them around your screen. Try it out! Just touch an app and drag your finger to move it. When you've found the perfect spot, lift your finger and the app drops into place. After you've downloaded more apps, you can also drag apps across home screens.

You can delete an app using the same method for moving them. The only difference is instead of moving them, you tap the X in the upper left corner of the icon. Don't worry about deleting something on accident. Apps are stored in the cloud. You can delete and install them as many times as you want; you don't have to pay again-- you just have to download them again.

Putting apps on different screens is helpful, but to be really organized you want to use folders. You can, for example, have a folder for all your game apps, finance apps, social apps. Whatever you want. You pick what to name it. If you want a "Apps I use on the toilet" folder, then you can absolutely have it!

To create a folder, just drag one app over another app you'd like to add into that folder.

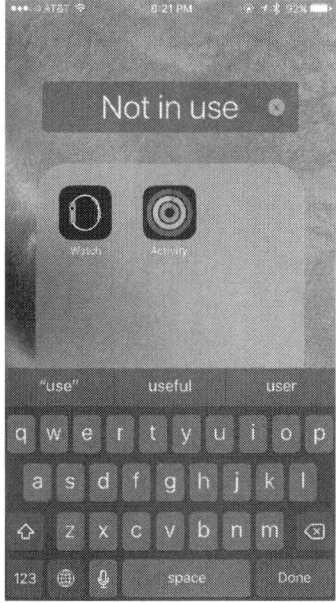

Once they are together, you can name the folder. To delete the folder, just put the folder apps in "jiggle mode" and drag them out of the folder. iPhone doesn't allow empty folders – when a folder is empty, iPhone deletes it automatically.

MESSAGING

More and more smartphone users are staying connected through text messages instead of phone calls,

42 | *The Ridiculously Simple Guide to iPhone X*

and the iPhone makes it easy to keep in touch with everyone. In addition to sending regular SMS text messages and multimedia messages (pictures, links, video clips and voice notes), you can also use iMessage to interact with other Apple users. This feature allows you to send instant messages to anyone signed into a Mac running OS X Mountain Lion or higher, or any iOS device running iOS 5 or greater. iMessage for iOS 11 has been completely changed to make everything just a little more…animated.

On the main Messages screen you will be able to see the many different conversations you have going on. You can also delete conversations by swiping from right to left on the conversation you'd like, and tapping the red delete button. New conversations or existing conversations with new messages will be highlighted with a big blue dot next to it, and the Message icon will have a badge displaying the number of unread messages you have, similar to the Mail and Phone icons.

To create a message, click on the Messages icon, then the Compose button in the top right corner.

Once the new message dialog box pops up, click on the plus icon to choose from your contacts list, or just type in the phone number of the person you wish to text. For group messages, just keep adding as many people as you'd like. Finally, click on the bottom field to begin typing your message.

iMessage has added in a lot of new features over the past few years. If all you want to do is send a message, then just tap the blue up arrow.

But you can do so much more than just send a message! (Please note, if you are sending a message with newer features to someone with an older OS or a non-Apple device, then it won't look as it appears on your screen).

To start with, go ahead and push (but don't release that blue button—or if you are using a phone with 3D Touch, press down a little firmer). This will bring up several different animations for the message.

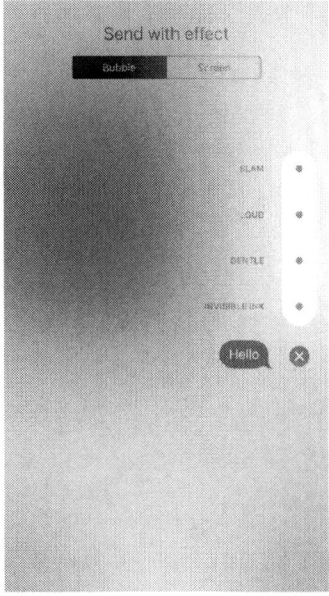

On the top of this screen, you'll also notice two tabs; one says "Bubble" and the other says "Screen"; if you tap "Screen" you can add animations to the entire screen. Swipe right and left to see each new animation.

When you get a message that you like and you want to respond to it, you can tap and hold your finger over the message or image; this will bring up different ways you can react.

Once you make your choice, the person on the receiving end will see how you responded.

If you'd like to add animation, a photo, a video, or lots of other things, then let's look at the options next to the message.

You have three choices--which bring up even more choices! The first is the camera, which let's you send photos with your message (or take new photos--note, these photos won't be saved on your phone), the next let's you used iMessage Apps (more on that in a second), and the last let's you record a message with your voice.

Let's look at the camera option first.

New Feature Alert! You can now add stickers, text, effects and more when you send someone a photo.

If you just want to attach a photo to your message, then after you tap the camera, go to the upper left corner and tap the photo icon; this brings up all the photos you can attach.

If you want to take an original photo, then tap the round button on the bottom. To add effects, tap the star in the lower left corner.

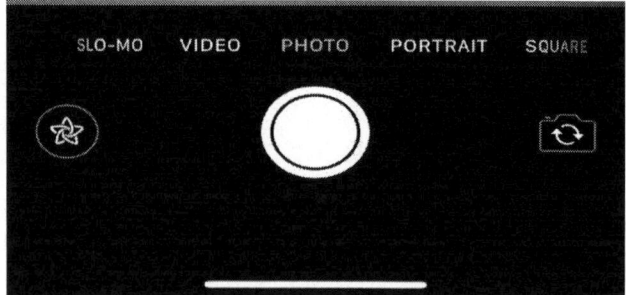

Tapping effects brings up all the different effects available to you. I'll talk more about Animoji soon but as an example, this app lets you put an Animoji over your face (see the example below--not bad for an author photo, eh?!)

Finally, the last option is apps. You should know all about phone apps by now, but now there's a new set of apps called iMessage apps. These apps let you be both silly (send digital stickers) or serious (send cash to someone via text). To get started, tap the plus sign to open the message app store.

You can browse all the apps just like you would the regular app store. Installing them is the same as well.

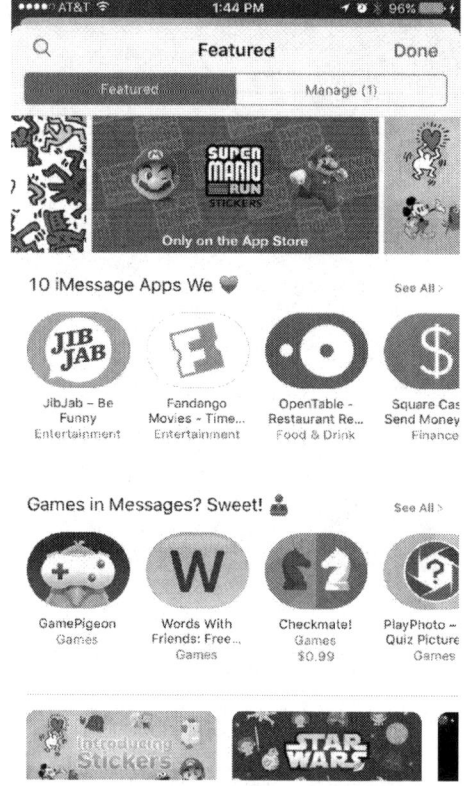

When your ready to use the app, just tap apps, tap the app you want to load, and tap what you want to send. You can also drag stickers on top of messages. Just tap, hold and drag.

Also in the app section is a button called #images.

If you tap on this button you can search for thousands of humorous meme's and animated GIFs. Just tap it and search a term you want to find—such as "Money" or "Fight".

One final iMessage feature worth trying out is the personal handwritten note. Tap on a new message like you are going to start typing a new message; now rotate your phone horizontal. This brings up an option to use your finger to create a handwritten note. Sign away, and then hit done when you're finished.

Notifications

When you have your phone locked, you'll start seeing notifications at some point; this tells you things like "You have a new email", "Don't forget to set your alarm", etc.

New Feature Alert: Notifications can get overwelming if you don't open your phone to clear them. iOS 12 introduced Grouping to notifications.

So when you see all your notifications on you lock screen, they'll be organized by what they are. To see all the notifications from any one category, just tap it.

Not a fan of Grouping? No problem. You can turn it off for any app. Head to Settings, then Notifications, then tap the app you want to turn grouping off for. Under Notification Groupings, just turn off automatic.

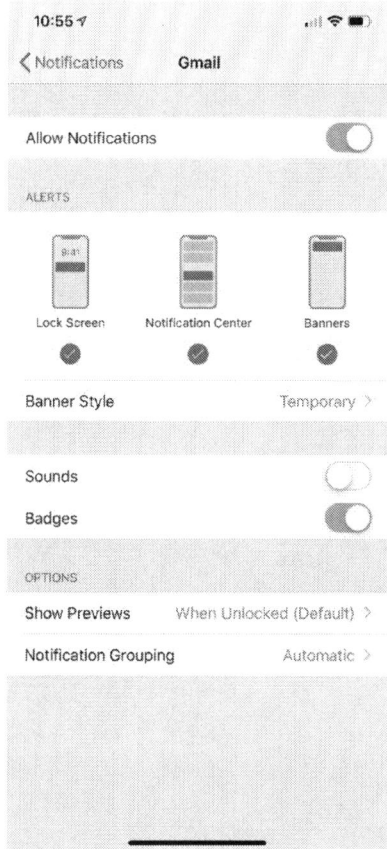

USING AIRDROP

AirDrop was introduced in iOS 7, though Apple fans have likely used the Mac OS version on MacBooks and iMacs. In Mac OSX Sierra and Yosemite, you'll finally be able to share between iOS and your Mac using AirDrop.

AirDrop is Apple's file sharing service, and it comes standard on iOS 12 devices. You can activate AirDrop from the Share icon anywhere in iOS 12. If other AirDrop users are nearby, you'll see anything they're sharing in AirDrop, and they can see anything you share.

AirDrop. Share instantly with people nearby. If they turn on AirDrop from Control Center on iOS or from Finder on the Mac, you'll see their names here. Just tap to share.

| Message | Mail | iCloud Photo Sharing | Notes | Twitter |

| Copy | Slideshow | AirPlay | Hide | Assign to Contact |

[4]
JUST THE BASICS...AND KEEP IT SIMPLE!

This chapter will cover:
- More about the Phone
- Sending Email
- Surfing the Web
- Using iTunes
- Apple Music
- Finding Apps on the App Store
- Adding Calendar Items
- Finding the Weather
- Using Maps
- iBooks
- Health
- Find My Friends
- Find My Phone
- HomeKit
- ARKit

There are millions of apps you can download, but Apple invests a lot of time making sure some of the best apps are there own. When you get a new iPhone, there are dozens of apps already installed. You're free to delete them (and later download them again), but before you do, make sure you know what they are.

PHONE

In previous chapters, you got a very high-level look at making calls. Now let's go a little deeper.

Open your Phone app. Notice the tabs on the bottom of the screen. Let's go over what each one does.

Favorites: These are the people you call most frequently. They are also in your contacts. It's kind of like your speed dial.

Recent: Any call (Outgoing or Incoming) will show up here. Incoming calls are in black, and outgoing calls are in red.

Contacts: This is where every contact will be. Do you notice the letters on the side? Tap the letter corresponding to the person you want to call to jump to that letter.

Keypad: This is what you use if you want to call the person using an actual keypad.

Voicemail: all your voicemail is stored here until you erase it.

Personally, I like to add contacts by going to icloud.com and signing in with my iTunes Account. It automatically syncs with the phone and is web-based which means that it doesn't matter whether you are using a Mac or a PC. I prefer this way because I can type with a real keyboard.

For the sake of this book, however, I am going to use the phone method; which is almost identical to the iCloud.

To add a contact, tap on 'Contacts', and then tap the '+' button in the upper right corner. Additionally, you can remove contacts by tapping on the edit button instead and then tapping on the person you want to delete, and then hitting delete.

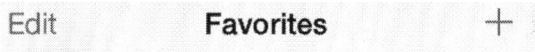

To insert information, all you need to do is tap in each field. If you tap on 'add photo' you will also have the option of taking someone's photo or using one you already have. If you want to assign a ringtone or a vibration, so that it plays a certain song only when this person is calling, then add that under ringtones. When you are finished, tap done. It will now give you the option of adding the person to your favorites if this is someone you will call often.

56 | *The Ridiculously Simple Guide to iPhone X*

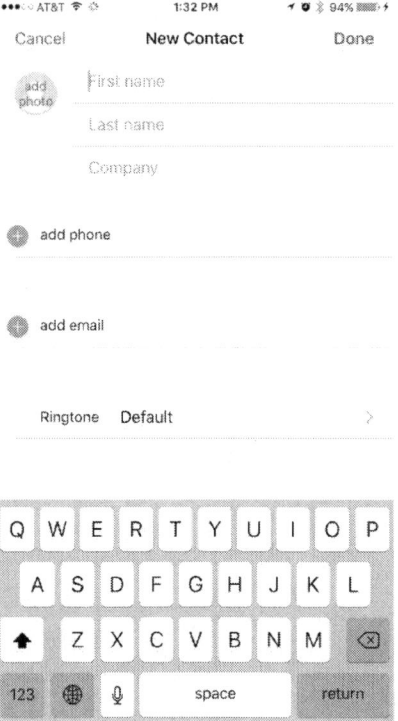

To call any person, simply tap their name. If you want to send them a text message instead, tap the blue arrow to the side of their name, note that only the blue arrow shows up if in the 'Favorites' section. To call someone not in your favorites, tap on their name in contacts and it will ask you if you want to call or text. If you prefer to call the person using Facetime (if they have Facetime) you will also have the option by tapping the blue exclamation button.

One highly advertised feature on the iPhone is 'Do Not Disturb'. When this feature is turned on, no calls get through; you don't even see that your phone ringing unless it's from someone in your approved list. That way you can have it set to ring only if someone in your family is calling. To use this feature, you need to go to your 'Settings' on your home screen.

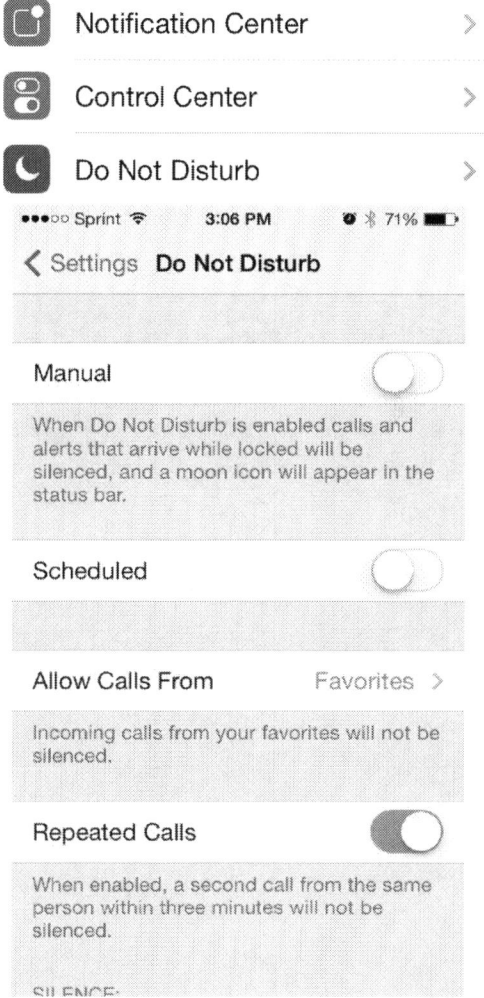

By default, when 'Do Not Disturb' is on, anyone in your favorites can call. Also, notice the 'Repeated Calls' button which is switched on by default. What that means is that if the same person calls twice in three minutes, it will go through.

If you want to set it to let no calls go through, tap on the 'Allow Calls From'. To get back to the previous menu, just tap the 'Do Not Disturb' button in the upper left corner. Anytime you see a button like that in the upper left corner, it means that it will take you to the previous screen. The information here saves as soon as you tap it, so don't worry about a save button.

Mail

The iPhone lets you add multiple email addresses from virtually any email client you can think of. Yahoo, Gmail, AOL, Exchange, Hotmail, and many more can be added to your phone so that you will be able to check your email no matter where you are. To add an email address, click on the Settings app icon, then scroll to the middle where you'll see Mail, Contacts & Calendar. You will then see logos for the biggest email providers, but if you have another type of email just click on "Other" and continue.

If you don't know your email settings, you will need to visit the Mail Settings Lookup page on the Apple website. There you can type in your entire email address, and the website will show you what information to type and where in order to get your email account working on the phone. The settings change with everyone, so what works for one provider may not work with another. Once you are finished adding as many email accounts as you may need, you will be able to click on the Mail app icon on your phone's home screen, and view each inbox separately, or all at once.

SURFING THE INTERNET WITH SAFARI

If you are using the iPhone, you probably already are paying for a data plan, so chances are you want to take full advantage of the Internet.

There's a good chance you are using a carrier that doesn't have unlimited web surfing. This means that if you use the Internet a lot, then you will have to pay extra. What I recommend is using Wi-Fi when you have it (like at home). So before we go back into 'Safari', let's look very quickly at how to enable Wi-Fi.

On your Home screen, tap the Settings icon.

The second option in the Settings menu is Wi-Fi; tap anywhere on that line once.

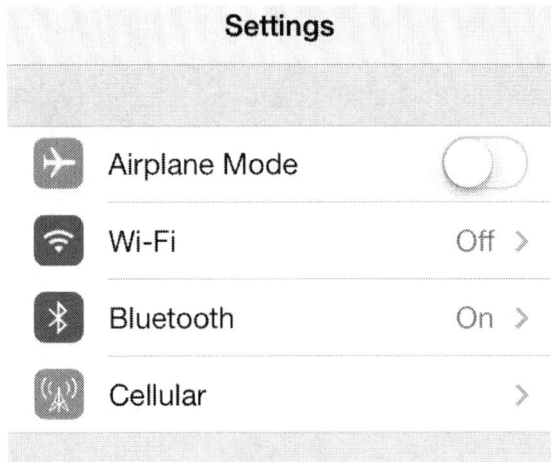

Next, switch the Wi-Fi from off to on by swiping or tapping on the 'Off'.

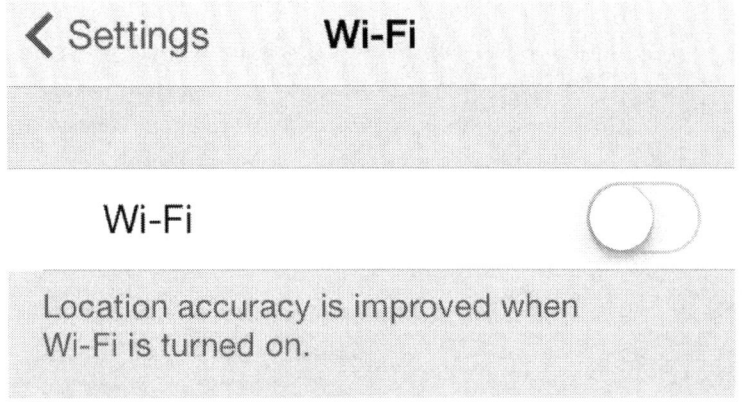

Your Wi-Fi network (if you have one) will now appear. Tap it once.

If there is a lock next to the signal symbol; that means the Wi-Fi access is locked and you need a password to use it. When prompted, type in the password and then tap 'Join'.

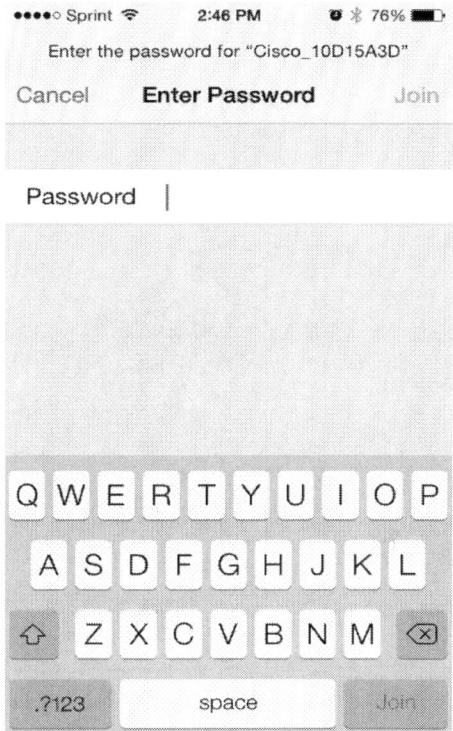

You will now connect to the network. Remember that many places, like Star Bucks, McDonalds, Nordstroms, Lowe's etc., offer free Wi-Fi as a way to entice you into the store and get you to stay. Take advantage of it and save data usage for the times you need it.

Let's see how Safari works.

Tap the 'Safari' icon once it will launch. You've already seen how the address bar works. To search for something you use the same exact box. That's how you can search for anything on the Internet. Think of it like a Google, Bing, or Yahoo! search engine in the corner of your screen. In fact, that's exactly what it is. Because when you search, it will use one of those search engines to find results.

On the bottom of the screen you'll see five buttons; the first two are back and forward buttons that makes the website go either backwards or forwards to the website you were previously on.

Next to the forward arrow, right in the middle, is a button that lets you share a website, add it to the 'Home Screen', print it, bookmark it, copy it, or add it to your reading list.

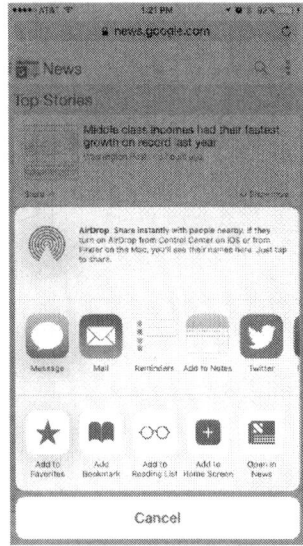

That's great! But what does it all mean? Let's look at each button on the menu:

Social Buttons: Mail, Message, Twitter, Facebook are 'Social Buttons'; pressing any of them will share the website you are looking at with whichever button you pressed (Message, FYI, is text message)

Add to Home Screen: If you go to a website frequently, this can be very convenient. What this button does is add an icon for that webpage right to your 'Home screen'. That way whenever you want to launch the website, you can do it directly from the 'Home screen'.

Print: If you have an AirPrint compatible printer, you can print a photo, document or webpage directly from your phone.

Copy: This copies the website address.

Bookmark: If you go to a website often but don't want to add it to your 'Home screen' then you can bookmark it. I will show you this in more detail in just a moment.

Add to Reading List: If you have a bunch of news stories open, you can add them to a Reading List to read later (even if you are offline).

The next button over, which looks like a book, is the bookmark button.

Let's go back to the bookmark button and see how that works.

When you add a bookmark (remember you do this from the previous button, the middle one), it will ask you to name it. By default it will put it in the general bookmarks tab, but you can also create new folders by clicking on 'Bookmarks'.

64 | *The Ridiculously Simple Guide to iPhone X*

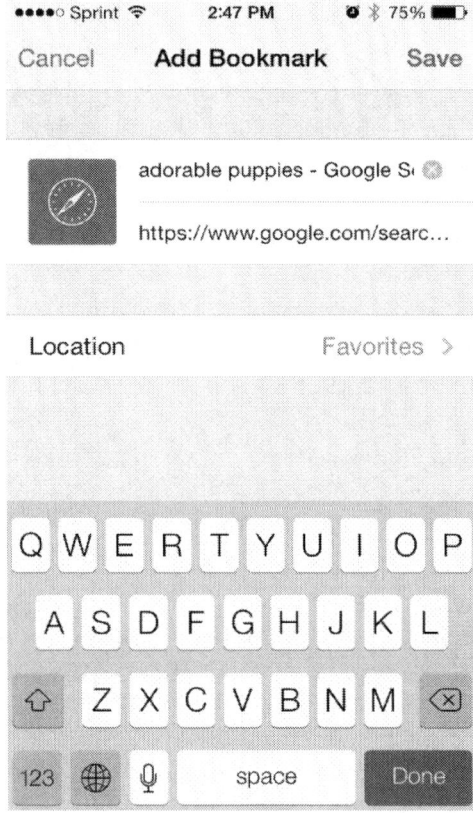

Now you can access the website anytime you want without typing the address by tapping on the Bookmarks button.

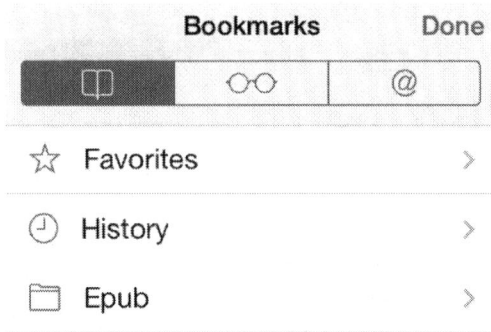

The iCloud tab is something you'll want to pay attention to if you use another Apple device (like an iPad, an iPod Touch or a Mac computer). Your safari browsing is automatically synced; so if you are browsing a page on your iPad, you can pick up where you left off on your iPhone.

The last button looks like a box on top of a transparent box.

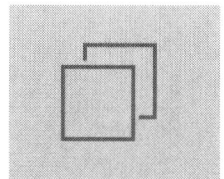

If you use a computer or an iPad; then you probably know all about tabs. Apple decided to not use tabs on 'Safari'. Tabs are there in another way though, that's what this button is; it lets you have several windows open at the same time. When you press it, a new window appears. There's an option to open a New Page. Additionally, you can toggle between the pages that you already have opened. Hitting the red 'x' will also close a page that you have opened. Hit done to go back to normal browsing.

When you put your phone in landscape (i.e. you turn it sideways), the browser also turns and you will now have the option to use Full-Screen mode. Tap the double arrows to activate it.

Reading list is the middle icon that looks like a pair of glasses where you can view all of the web pages, blog posts, or articles that you've saved for offline reading. To save a piece of internet literature to your reading list, tap on the Share icon and then click on Add to Reading List. Saved pages can be deleted like a text message by swiping from right to left and tapping on the red Delete button.

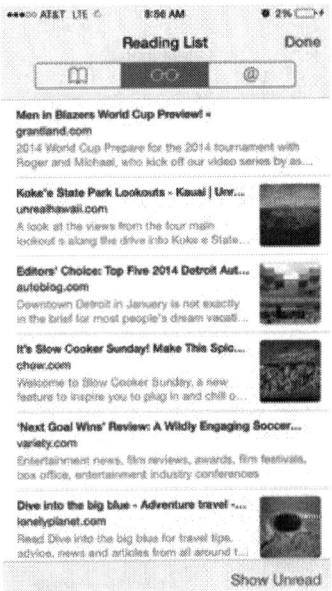

The third tab on the Bookmarks page is where you can view your shared links and subscriptions. Subscriptions can be created from any web page that provides RSS feeds, and your phone will automatically download the latest articles and posts. To subscribe to a site's RSS, visit the website, tap the Bookmark icon, and select Add to Shared Links.

Back on the main Safari home page, the last button found on the bottom right corner is Tabs. Just like the Mac version you can have multiple tabs of web pages open at the same time, and switch between them with ease. To switch the tabs into private mode where your browsing history or cookies will not be saved or recorded, tap the Tabs button and select Private. You will be asked to either close all existing tabs or keep them. If you don't want to lose any tabs that might still be open, opt to keep them. Existing tabs, in addition to any new tabs you open, will now be shielded behind private browsing.

ITUNES

The iTunes app found on your home screen opens the biggest digital music store in the world. You will be able to purchase and download not just music, but also countless movies, TV shows, audiobooks, and more. On the iTunes home page, you can also find a What's Hot section, collections of music, and new releases.

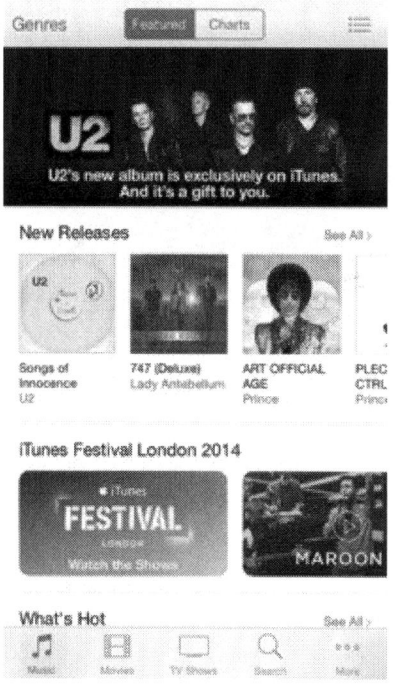

At the top, you will see the option to view either featured media or browse through the top charts. On the upper left corner is the Genres button. Clicking Genres will bring up many different types of music to help refine your search.

New Feature Alert: When you search a lyric in iTunes, it now brings back results.

Apple Music

Apple Music, is a relatively new service from Apple that gives you the ability to stream the entire iTunes store and receive curated playlists from music experts tailored to your preferences. It costs $9.99 a month, but you can take advantage of the three-month free trial to see if this service is for you before paying for it. It also offers discount subscription pricing for family plans and college students.

Buying Apps

So how do you buy, download and finally remove apps? I'll look at that in this section.

To purchase apps, and I don't actually mean paying for them because you can buy a free app without paying for it, follow the following:

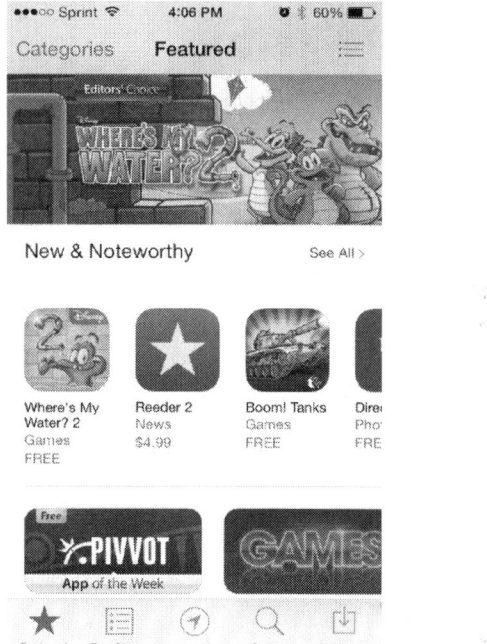

The first thing you see when you open the app store are the feature apps. This is to say games, lots and lots of games! Games are the top telling category in the app store, but don't worry, there is more there than just games. Later in this handbook, I will tell you some of the essential apps you should get, but for now, let's see how the app store works so that you discover some of them yourself.

In the top left corner of both the 'featured' page and the 'top charts' (to get to the top charts, tap on the button on the bottom) is a button that says 'Categories'. This is how you can break down the apps into non-game categories.

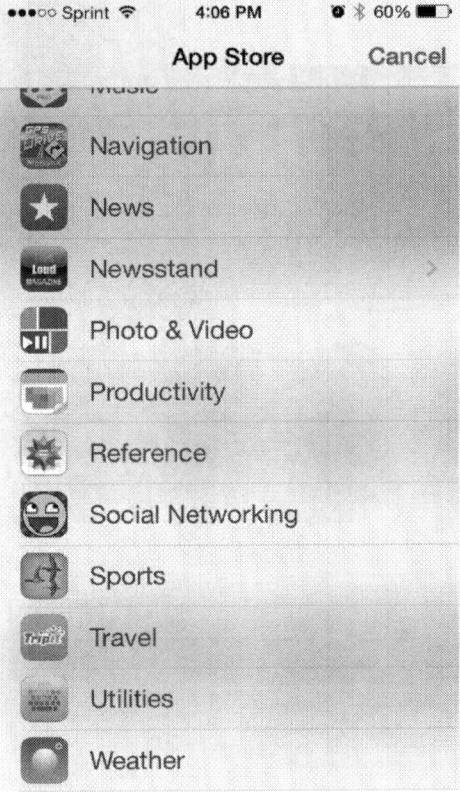

If you hear about a new app and want to check it out, use the 'Search' option.

When you find an app you want to buy, simply tap the price button and type in your App store password. Remember that just because an app is free to download doesn't mean you won't have to pay something to use it. Many apps use 'in-app purchases' which means that you have to buy something within the app. You will be notified before you purchase anything though.

Apps are constantly coming out with updates like new, better features. Updates are almost always free, unless noted, and are easy to install. Just click on the last tab: 'updates'. If you have any apps that need to be updated, you will see it here. You will also see what's new in the app. If you see one, tap 'update' to begin the update.

If you bought an app, but accidentally deleted it, or changed your mind about deleting it, don't worry! You can download the app again in the same place that you see the updates. Just tap on 'Purchased'.

When you tap the 'Purchased' button, you will see two options: one is to see all the apps you have purchased and one to just see the apps that you have purchased but are not on your phone. Tap the one that says 'Not on This iPhone' to re-download anything, at no cost. Just tap the Cloud button to the right of the screen. You can even download it again if you bought it on another iPhone as long as it's under the same account.

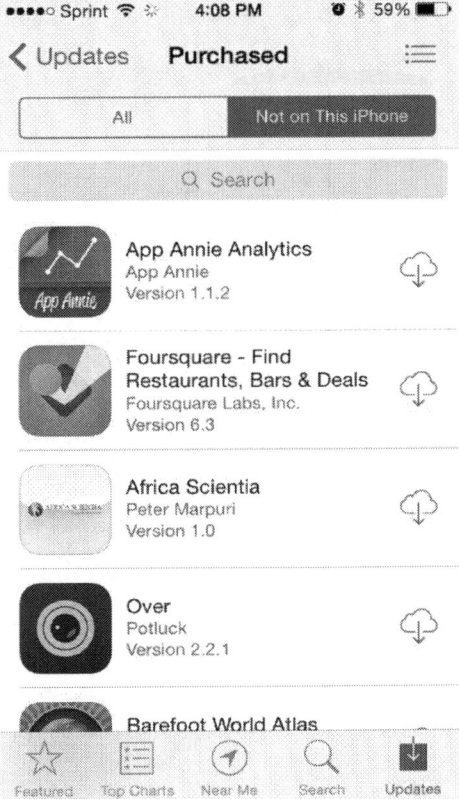

Deleting apps is easy; on your 'home' screen, tap and hold the icon of the app you want to remove, then tap the 'x' on top of the app.

CALENDAR

Among the other pre-installed apps that came with your new iPhone, perhaps one of the most used apps you'll encounter is the calendar. You can switch between viewing appointments, tasks, or everything laid out in a one day, one week, or one month view. On the iPhone 6 Plus, turn your phone on its side and you will notice everything switch to landscape mode. A first for the iPhone, many new apps now take advantage of the larger iPhone's 1080p resolution by displaying more information at once, similar to the iPad and iPad mini display. Combine your calendar with email accounts or iCloud to keep your appointments and tasks synced across all of your devices, and never miss another appointment.

Creating an Appointment

To create an appointment, click on the Calendar icon on your home screen. Click on whichever day you would like to set the appointment for, and then tap the plus sign (+) in the corner. Here you will be able to name and edit your event, as well as connect it to an email or iCloud account in order to allow for syncing.

76 | *The Ridiculously Simple Guide to iPhone X*

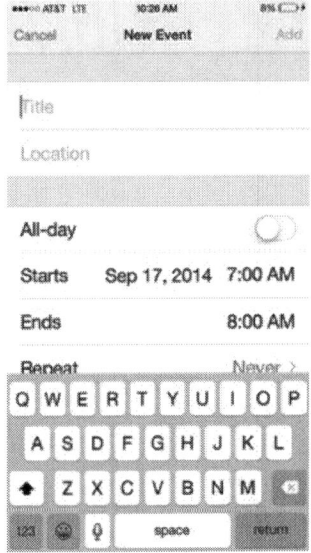

When editing your event, pay special attention to the duration of your event. Select the start and end times, or choose "All Day" if it's an all-day event. You will also have a chance to set it as a recurring event by clicking on Repeat and selecting how often you want it to repeat. In the case of a bill or car payment, for example, you could either select Monthly (on this day) or every 30 days, which are two different things. After you select your repetition, you can also choose how long you'd like for that event to repeat itself: for just one month, a year, forever, and everything in between.

WEATHER

You can use your iPhone's location services and GPS to help you navigate to your destinations, but other apps can use it to display localized information. The Weather app is one such example of this. Opening it up will immediately show you basic weather information based on your current location. To get more detailed information, you can swipe left and right on the middle section to scroll through the hourly forecast, and swipe up and down on the bottom section to scroll through the 10 day forecast.

You can add more cities by clicking on the list icon towards the bottom right and searching for the city name. Once you've added cities, you can scroll between cities to see real-time weather information for each location by swiping left or right, and the number of cities you have added are shown at the bottom in the form of small dots.

78 | The Ridiculously Simple Guide to iPhone X

Maps

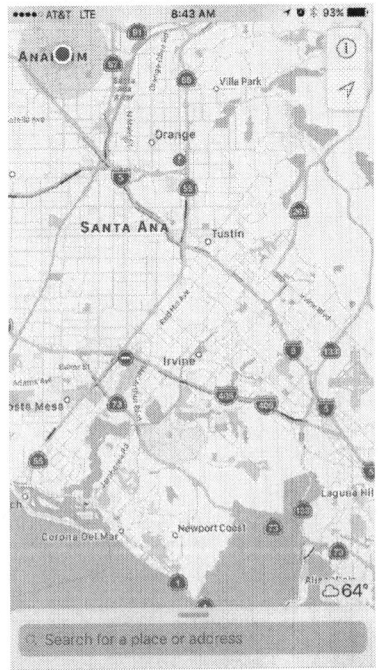

The Maps app is back and better than ever. After Apple parted ways with Google Maps several years ago, Apple decided to develop its own, made-for-iPhone map and navigation system. The result is a beautiful travel guide that takes full advantage of the newest iPhone resolutions. Full screen mode allows every corner of the phone to be filled with the app, and there's an automatic night mode just like with iBooks. You'll be able to search for places, restaurants, gas stations, concert halls, and other venues near you at any time, and turn-by-turn navigation is available for walking, biking, driving, or commuting. Traffic is updated in real time, so if an accident occurs ahead of you or there is construction going on, Maps will offer a faster alternative and warn you of the potential traffic jam.

The turn-by-turn navigation is easy to understand without being distracting, and the 3D view makes potentially difficult scenarios (like highway exits that come up abruptly) much more pleasant. Another convenient feature is the ability to avoid highways and toll roads entirely.

To set up navigation, tap on the Maps icon. On the bottom of the screen is a search for place or address; for homes you need an address, but businesses just need a name. Click on it and enter your destination once prompted.

When you find your destination's address, click on Route, and choose between walking or driving directions. For businesses, you also have the option of reading reviews and calling the company directly.

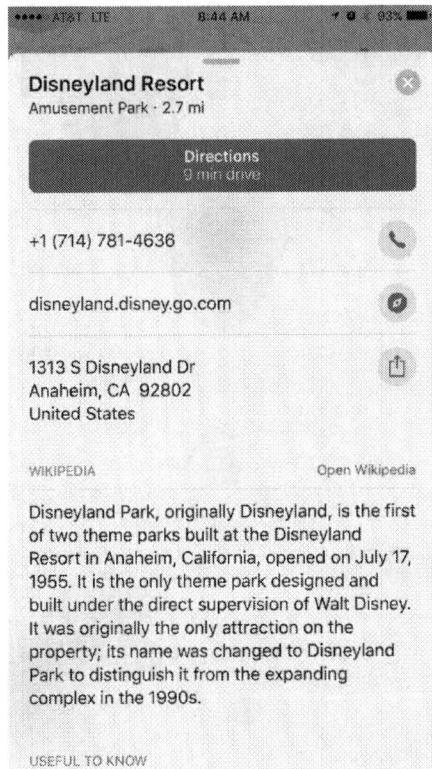

For hands-free navigation, press and hold the home button to enable Siri (which will be discussed in the next section) and say "Navigate to" or "Take me to" followed by the address or name of the location that you'd like to go to.

If you'd like to avoid highways or tolls, simply tap the more options button and select the option that you want.

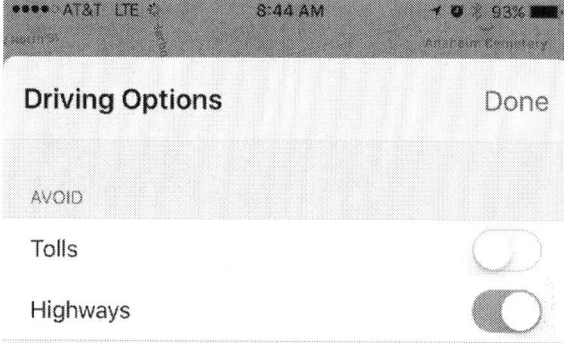

Apple Maps also let's you see a 3D view of thousands of locations. To enable this option, tap the "i" in the upper right corner. After this, select satellite view.

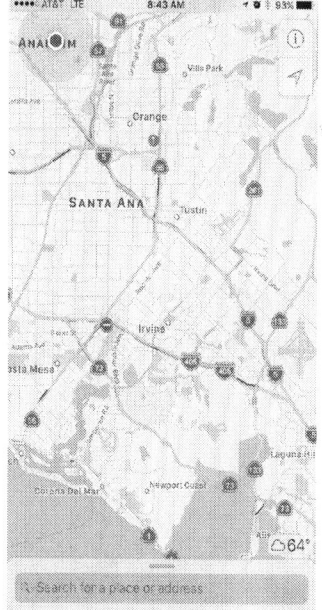

If 3D view is available you'll notice a change immediately. You can use two fingers to make your map more or less flat. You can also select 2D to remove 3D altogether.

iBooks

Now that the iPhone features bigger screens (iPhone 6 and up), you can probably do more and more reading on your phone while reading less on your iPad. If that's the case, you will love the new version of iBooks. Your favorite books can be read in complete full screen mode, and flick through the pages to enjoy that classic page-turning animation. Trying to organize your library and keep track of which books you have left to complete a book series? Now iBooks automatically sorts books by series, keeping everything neat and tidy for you.

The latest updates enable you to upload quotes directly to your favorite social networking or blogging site, and if you see a word you aren't familiar with, just press and hold it until the word in question becomes highlighted, then select Dictionary. Additionally, night time reading has gotten easier with the night theme. Dim or shut the lights off while reading and iBooks will automatically switch to night mode for easier viewing. Turn the lights back on, and the theme will switch back to normal reading mode.

HEALTH

The release of the latest iPhone models brought with it a much greater focus on one's health, and as such, the new iPhones come with the Health app. The Health app keeps track of many different things pertaining to your health, including calories burned, your weight, heart rate, body measurements, and even an emergency card that lets you store important health information such as your blood type and allergies in the event of an emergency. There are four different tabs at the bottom of the app:

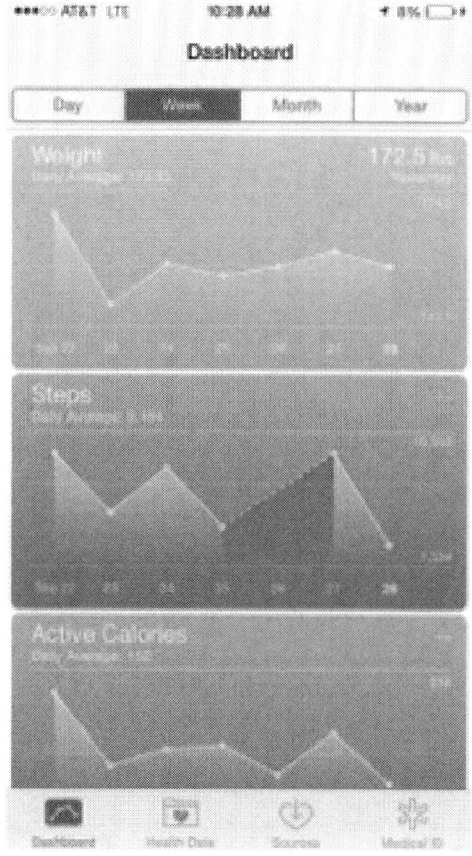

Dashboard

Here you will be able to see an at-a-glance view of your vitals, including calories burned, weight, and heart rate. You will be able to choose between one day's worth of information, a week, month, and even a year if you'd like to see how your health today compares to last year.

Health Data

This page is the main hub where you can find and store all of your information. It's broken down into a few general categories like body measurements, fitness, nutrition, sleep, and vitals, but can include even the smallest details like your blood sugar level, glucose levels, sleep patterns, current medications, and more.

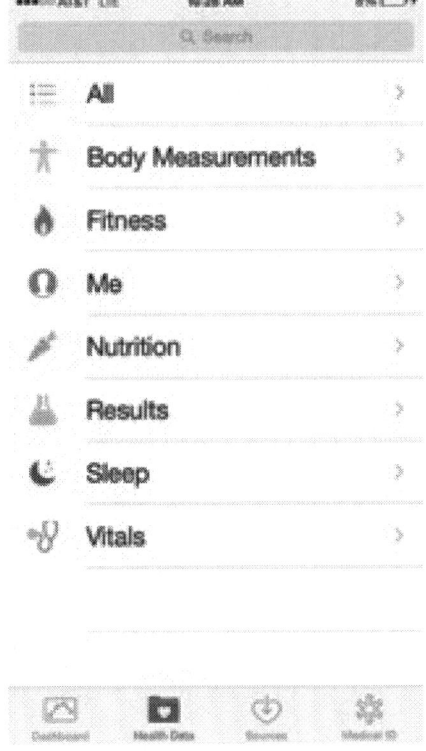

Sources

Sources weren't available at launch, but it's finally been released to much acclaim. This section is where you can control who or what can access your health information, as well as who can send you information regarding your health.

It's meant to connect to third party apps or doctors in order to send them accurate information about you, and a quick snapshot of how your days are even when you aren't visiting the doctor. This could be especially beneficial to you if you have a health condition that requires more frequent monitoring, such as diabetes.

Medical ID

Here is the virtual emergency card we mentioned earlier. This is the place to store all the important information about you in case a medical worker needs it in the event of an emergency. Enter in your blood type, allergies (medical or otherwise), chronic health conditions, diseases, medications, emergency contact, and anything else you can think of so whoever is treating you can access revenant information without wasting time.

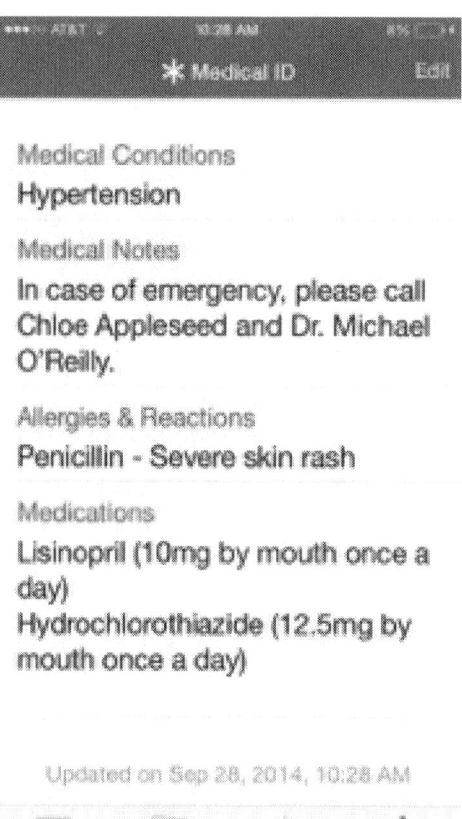

Find My Friends

Find My Friends is a social people finder app that can also be run as a widget in your Notifications center. The app displays a map that shows exactly where your friends are and how far away they are from you. You'll have to add friends using the Add function in the top right corner, and your friends will have to approve the service. You can even set up notifications that alert you when a friend leaves or arrives at a specified location by tapping a friend's icon in the app and then tapping Notify Me.

Find iPhone

Find iPhone is a useful app that allows you to see the location of all of your Apple devices on a map. You can remotely play sounds on devices (to help you find them under a pile of laundry, for example), send messages to them, and remotely erase them in case of theft. Of course, the app that's installed on your iPhone won't help you find your iPhone, but if your phone goes missing and you don't have any other Apple devices, just log on to icloud.com to see where your device has wandered to.

Home

We may have saved the best app for last with the newest app to launch in iOS 12 – Home. The Home app integrates HomeKit with iOS to help you better integrate all your home appliances and utilities, like lights, thermostats, refrigerators, and more. HomeKit uses Siri to control all of your smart home devices, which is a pretty handy tool, and the Home interface allows for a much cleaner and straight forward experience. To add your smart home device to Home, simply stand next to it with its power on and your Home app enabled. You can also use your 4th generation Apple TV to control HomeKit-enabled smart home devices. HomePod is something else that is housed here.

ARKIT

iPhone is all about augmented reality; they see this as the future. Many new apps have AR support.

New Feature Alert: ARKit for iOS 12 introduced a new measurements tool.

To use the new measurements tool, open the Measure app. Point your camera at a rectangle option, and watch a box automatically form over it.

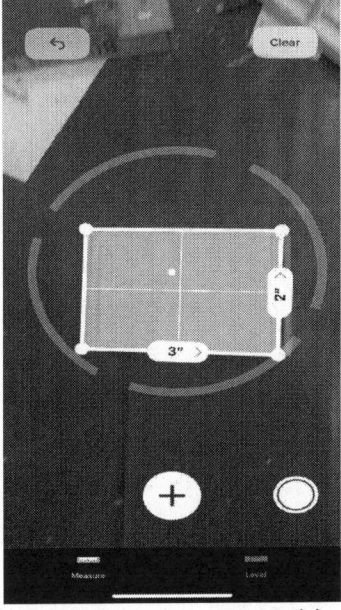

The app will tell you how long something is, and also allow you to add points, so you can measure it as well.

[5]
Make It Yours

This chapter will cover:
- Screen Time
- Do Not Disturb Mode
- Notifications and Widgets
- General Settings
- Sounds
- Customizing Brightness and Wallpaper
- Adding Facebook, Twitter and Flickr Accounts
- Family Sharing
- Continuity and Handoff

Now that you know your way around, it's time to dig into the settings and make this phone completely custom to you!

For most of this chapter, I'll be hanging out in the Settings area, so if you aren't already there, tap Settings from your Home screen.

Screen Time

> **New Feature Alert:** Screen Time lets you see just how much time you spend on your phone, and doing what. You may be surprised--heck, you may not even want to know about this feature! You can also use it to monitor the amount of time you kids spend on their devices.

To use Screen Time, head on into Settings > Screen Time

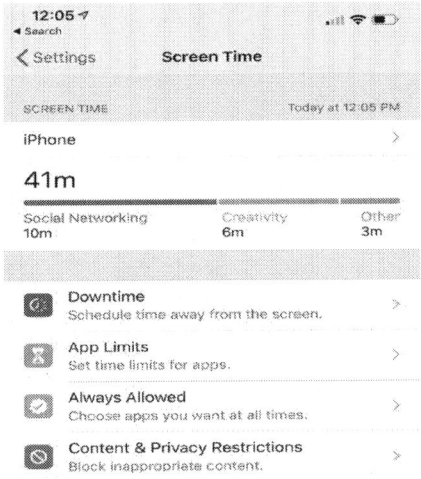

According to the image above, I've been on my phone 41 minutes; that's not too bad...but I've only had my phone on for 42!

You can click on any app to see how much time you've spent in it, and even what your average is. From here you can also add limits.

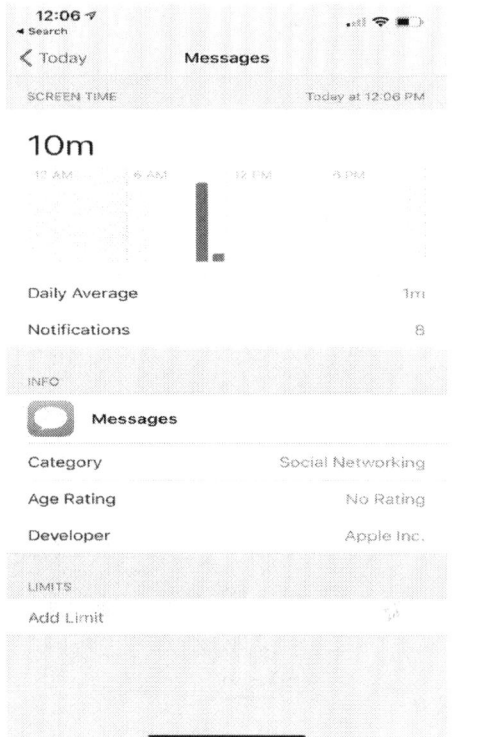

Do Not Disturb Mode

Do Not Disturb mode is a handy feature located near the top of your Settings app. When this operational mode is enabled, you won't receive any notifications and all of your calls will be silenced. This is a useful trick for those times when you can't afford to be distracted (and let's face it, your iPhone is as communicative as they come, and sometimes you'll need to have some peace and quiet!). Clock alarms will still sound.

To turn on, schedule and customize Do Not Disturb, just tap on Do Not Disturb in Settings. You can schedule automatic times to activate this feature, like your work hours, for example. You can also specify certain callers who should be allowed when your phone is set to Do Not

Disturb. This way, your mother can still get through, but you won't have to hear every incoming email. To do this, use the Allow Call From command in Do Not Disturb settings.

Do Not Disturb is also accessible through the Control Center (swipe up from the bottom of the screen to access it at any time).

Notifications and Widgets

Notifications are one of the most useful features on the iPhone, but chances are you won't need to be informed of every single event that's set as a default in your Notifications Center. To adjust Notifications preferences, go to Settings > Notifications.

By tapping the app, you can turn Notifications off or on and finesse the type of notification from each app. It's a good idea to whittle this list down to the apps that you truly want to be notified from – for example, if you're not an investor, turn off Stocks! Reducing the number of sounds your iPhone makes can also reduce phone-related frazzledness. For example, in Mail, you may want your phone to make a sound when you receive email from someone on your VIP list but to only display badges for other, less important email.

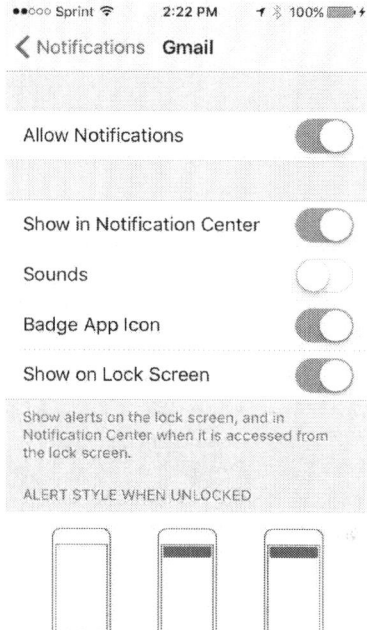

GENERAL SETTINGS

The General menu item is a little bit of a catchall. This is where you'll find information about your iPhone, including its current version of iOS and any available software updates. Fortunately, iOS 12 ushers in an era of smaller, more efficient updates, so you won't find yourself scrambling to delete apps in order to make space for the latest improvements. You can also check your phone and iCloud storage here.

The Accessibility options are located here as well. You can set your iPhone according to your needs with Zoom, Voiceover, large text, color adjustment, and more. There are a quite a few Accessibility options that can make iOS 12 easy for everyone to use, including Grayscale View and improved Zoom options.

VoiceOver	Off >
Zoom	Off >
Invert Colors	◯
Grayscale	◯
Speech	>
Larger Text	Off >
Bold Text	◯
Button Shapes	◯
Increase Contrast	>
Reduce Motion	Off >
On/Off Labels	◯

A handy Accessibility option that's a little disguised is the Assistive Touch setting. This gives you a menu that helps you access device-level functions. Enabling it brings up a floating menu designed to help users who have difficulty with screen gestures like swiping or with manipulating the iPhone's physical buttons. Another feature for those with visual needs is Magnifier. Turning this on allows your camera to magnify things, and you can also click the home button and magnify anything that you're looking at.

We recommend taking some time and tapping through the General area, just so you know where everything is!

SOUNDS

Hate that vibration when your phone rings? Want to change your ring tone? Head to the Sounds Settings menu! Here you can turn vibration on or off and assign ring tones to a number of iPhone functions. We do suggest finding an isolated space before you start trying out all the different sound settings – it's fun, but possibly a major annoyance to those unlucky enough not to be playing with their own new iPhone!

Tip: You can apply individual ringtones and message alerts to your contacts. Just go to the person's contact screen in Contacts, tap Edit, and tap Assign Ringtone.

Customizing Brightness and Wallpaper

On the iPhone, wallpaper refers to the background image on your home screen and to the image displayed when your iPhone is locked (lock screen). You can change either image using two methods.

For the first method, visit Settings > Wallpapers. You'll see a preview of your current wallpaper and lock screen here. Tap Choose a New Wallpaper. From there, you can choose a pre-loaded dynamic (moving) or still image, or choose one of your own photos. Once you've chosen an image, you'll see a preview of the image as a lock screen. Here, you can turn off Perspective Zoom, which makes the image appear to shift as you tilt your phone) if you like. Tap Set to continue. Then choose whether to set the image as the lock screen, home screen, or both.

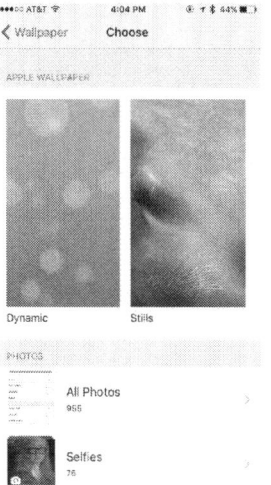 

The other way to make the change is through your Photo app. Find the photo you'd like to set as a wallpaper image and tap the Share button. You'll be given a choice to set an image as a background, a lock screen, or both.

If you want to use images from the web, it's fairly easy. Just press and hold the image until the Save Image / Copy / Cancel message comes up. Saving the image will save it to your Recently Added photos in the Photos app.

PRIVACY

The Privacy heading in Settings lets you know what apps are doing with your data. Every app you've allowed to use Location Services will show up under Location Services (and you can toggle Location Services off and on for individual apps or for your whole device here as well). You can also go through your apps to check what information each one is receiving and transmitting.

MAIL, CONTACTS, CALENDARS SETTINGS

If you need to add additional mail, contacts or calendar accounts, tap Settings > Mail, Contacts and Calendars to do so. It's more or less the same process as adding a new account in-app. You can also adjust other settings here, including your email signature for each linked account. This is also a good place to check which aspects of each account are linked – for example, you may want to link your Tasks, Calendars and Mail from Exchange, but not your Contacts. You can manage all of this here.

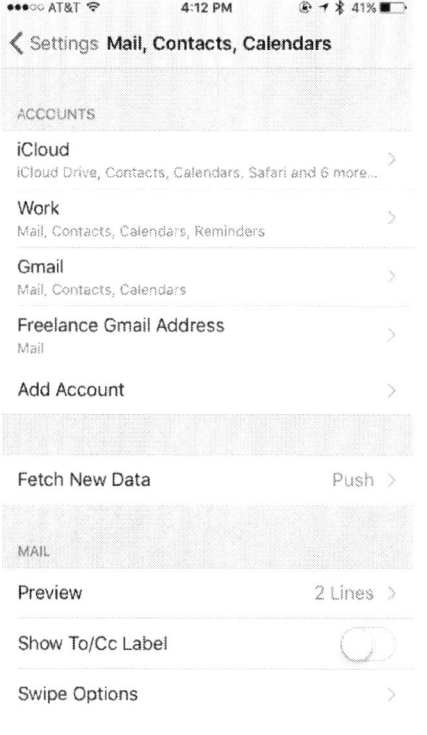

There are a number of other useful settings here, including the frequency you want your accounts to check for mail (Push, the default, being the hardest on your battery life). You can also turn on features like Ask Before Deleting and adjust the day of the week you'd like your calendar to start on.

Adding Facebook and Twitter

If you use Twitter, Facebook or Flickr, you'll probably want to integrate them with your iPhone. This is a snap to do. Just tap on Settings and look for Twitter, Facebook and Flickr in the main menu (you can also integrate Vimeo and Weibo accounts if you have them). Tap on the platform you want to integrate. From there, you'll enter your user name and password. Doing this will allow you to share webpages, photos, notes, App Store pages, music and more straight from your iPhone's native apps.

iPhone will ask you if you'd like to download the free Facebook, Twitter and Flickr apps when you configure your accounts if you haven't already done so. We recommend doing this – the apps are easy to use, free, and look great.

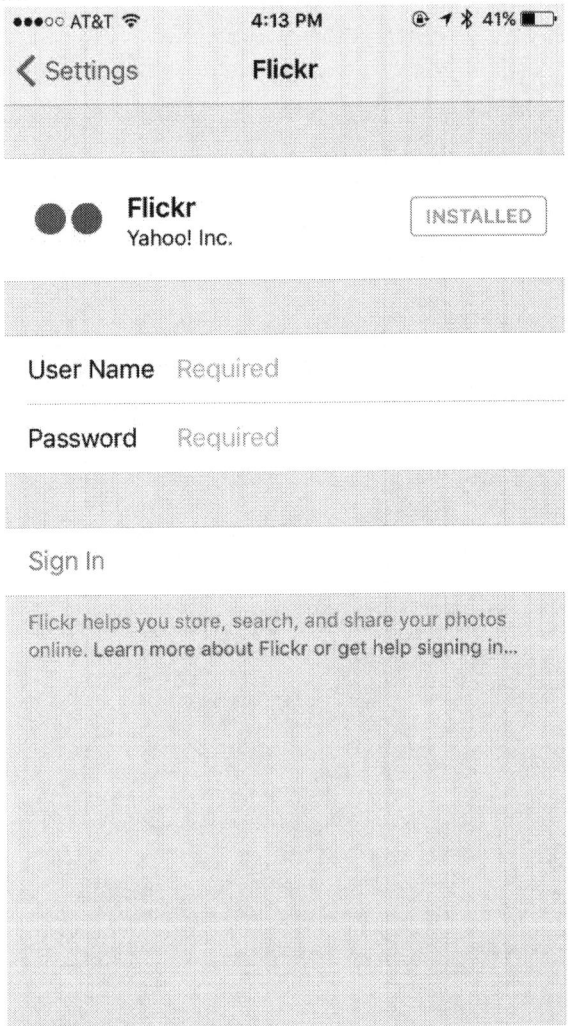

We found that when we associated our Facebook accounts, our contact list got extremely bloated. If you don't want to include your Facebook friends in your contacts list, adjust the list of applications that can access your Contacts in Settings > Facebook.

FAMILY SHARING

Family Sharing is one of our favorite iOS 12 features. Family Sharing allows you to share App Store and iTunes purchases with family members (previously, accomplishing this required a tricky and not-entirely-in-compliance-with-terms-of-service dance). Turning on Family Sharing also creates a shared family calendar, photo album, and reminder list. Family members can also see each other's location in Apple's free Find My Friends app and check the location of each other's devices in the free Find iPhone app. Overall, Family Sharing is a great way to keep everyone entertained and in sync! You can include up to six people in Family Sharing.

To enable Family Sharing, go to Settings > iCloud. Here, tap Set Up Family Sharing to get started. The person who initiates Family Sharing for a family is known as the family organizer. It's an important role, since every purchase made by family members will be made using the family organizer's credit card! Once you set up your family, they'll also be able to download your past purchases, including music, movies, books, and apps.

Invite your family members to join Family Sharing by entering their Apple IDs. As a parent, you can create Apple IDs for your children with parental consent. When you create a new child Apple ID, it is automatically added to Family Sharing.

There are two types of accounts in Family Sharing – adult and child. As you'd expect, child accounts have more potential restrictions than adult accounts do. Of special interest is the Ask to Buy option. This prevents younger family members from running up the family organizer's credit card bill by requiring parental authorization for purchases. The family organizer can also designate other adults in the family as capable of authorizing purchases on children's devices.

If you'd like to further lock down your children's iOS devices, be sure to take a look at 5.2 for information about setting up additional restrictions!

Continuity and Handoff

iOS 12 includes some incredible features for those of us who work on multiple iOS 12 and Sierra and Yosemite OSX devices. Now, when your computer is running Yosemite or higher or your iOS 12 iPad is connected to the same Wi-Fi network as your iOS 12 iPhone, you can answer calls or send text messages (both iMessages and regular SMS messages) from your iPad or computer.

The Handoff feature is present in apps like Numbers, Safari, Mail and many more. Handoff allows you to leave an app in one device mid-action and pick up right where you left off on a different device. It makes life much easier for those of us living a multi-gadget lifestyle.

[6]
LIGHTS, CAMERA, ACTION

This chapter will cover:
- Taking photos and videos
- Editing photos
- Sharing photos and videos

TAKING PHOTOS AND VIDOES

Now that you know how to make a phone call, let's get back to the fun stuff! I'll look at using the photo app next.

The camera app is on your 'Home' screen, but you can also access it from your 'lock' screen for quick, easy access.

The camera app is pretty simple to use. First, you should know that the camera app has two cameras; one on the front and one on the back.

The front camera has a lower resolution and is mostly used for self-portraits; it still takes excellent photos, but just remember the back camera is better. To access it, tap the button in the top right corner (the one with the camera and two arrows). The bar on the bottom has all your camera modes. This is how you can switch from photo to video mode.

In the upper-left corner of the screen you will see a lightening button. That's your flash. Tap this button and you can toggle between different flash modes.

If you want to take higher definition photographs; (Note: all video is already HD), then you'll want to turn 'HDR' on.

The last three buttons you won't use quite as much. The first, the circle, is for live photos; live photos takes a short video while you take the photo; it's so quick you won't even know it did it; it's on automatically, so tap it once to turn it off; if you tap and hold a photo with live photo enabled, then you will see the video. Next to that is a timer, which, as you might expect, delays the shot so you can take a group photo. And finally the last button let's you add different colors to the photo.

One of the photo modes is called "Pano" or Panorama. Panorama is the ability to take an extra long photo that's over 20 megapixels in size. To use it tap the 'Panorama' button. On screen instructions will now appear. Simply press the 'Shoot' button at the bottom of the screen, and rotate the camera as straight as possible while following the line. When it reaches the end, the photo will automatically go into your album.

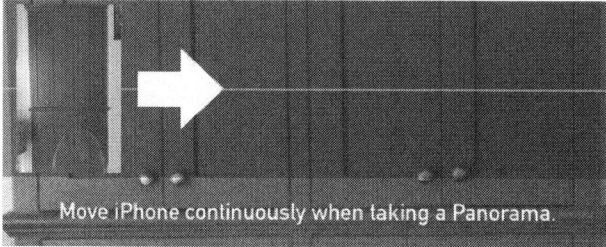

The mode you've probably seen the most about is Portrait Mode. Portrait Mode gives your photos that blurred effect you see on high-end DSLR cameras.

Whether a user is a selfie lover or a photo portrait addict, these are two features all users will appreciate.

To access and use portrait mode and portrait light mode in X or 8+:
1. Bring up the camera app.
2. Swipe left or right to switch to the Portrait setting.
3. Line up the shot within 2-8 feet of the subject. The camera's face and body detection will automatically identify the subject and provide instruction to move further or get closer to the subject.

4. Pay attention to the Camera app's prompts: More light required, flash may help, place subject within 8 feet, or move farther away.
5. When the shot is ready a banner will appear at the bottom.
6. Swipe or tap on the cube icons above the shutter button to change lighting effects.
7. Press the shutter button to take the photo.

Note: Users can still shoot with the telephoto lens in Portrait mode even if the banners don't turn yellow — it just means a lesser depth or lighting effect.

There's several different Portrait Modes (studio lighting, for example), but you can switch modes after you take the photo; so if you take it with Studio Lighting, but decide another mode would look better, then you can change it.

New Feature Alert: The newest iPhones can now adjust the depth of the blur after the photo is taken. To do this, just select Edit after the shot is taken. This only works for photos taken with Portrait Mode.

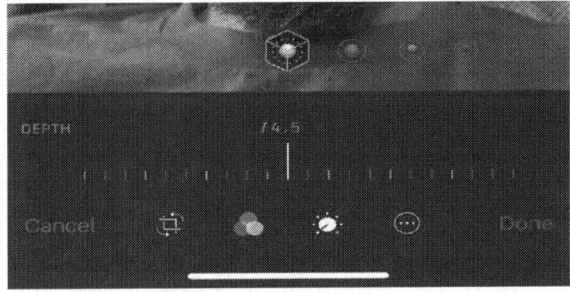

PHOTO EDITING

Editing your photos is just as easy as taking them. As simple as editing tools are, they are also quite powerful. If you want more power though, you can always download one of the hundreds of photo editing apps in the app store.

To edit a photo, tap the 'Photo' icon on your 'Home' screen.

When you launch 'Photos', you will see a tab with three buttons; right now, I'll be talking about the 'Photos button, but we'll talk about 'Photo Stream' in the next chapter. Tap albums and let's get editing!

Next, tap the photo you want to edit and then tap 'edit' in the upper-right corner. This will open the editing menu. On the bottom of the screen, you will see all the options: undo, auto correct (which corrects the color of the photo), color change, red eye removal, and finally crop.

The only added feature is the middle one, which let's you change the color saturation.

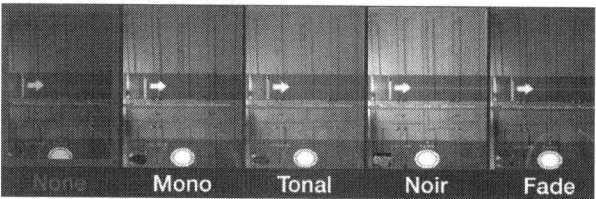

When you are satisfied with the changes tap save in the upper right corner.

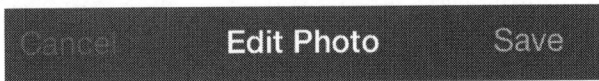

Remember whenever you want to get to the previous screen just tap the back button in the upper-left corner.

EDITING LIVE PHOTOS

Apple introduced Live Photos in 2015, when the iPhone 6s came out. This feature enhances the smartphone's photography, using pictures that move when you perform a 3D Touch on them. iOS 12 makes Live Photos better than ever. Wanna know how to take a live photo? Let's have a look.

Live Photos records what happens 1.5 seconds before and after you take the photo. That means you're not only getting a photo, you're also getting movement and sound.

Open the Camera app

Set your camera to photo mode, and turn Live Photos on

Hold the phone very still

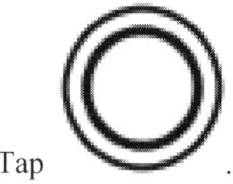

Tap .

With your iPhone 8 and up, Live Photos is naturally on by default. If you want to take a still image, tap and you'll be allowed to turn off Live Photos. If you want Live Photos to always be off, go to Settings > Camera > Preserve Settings.

Photo Albums and Photo Sharing

So now that your photo is taken and edited, let's see how to share photos.

There are several ways to share photos. When you open a photo, you will see an option bar on the bottom. The older version had more options—these options have now been moved to one central place, which you will see next.

The first button lets you share the photo socially and to media devices..

The top row is more of the social options; the bottom row is more of the media options. AirPlay, for example, let's you wirelessly send the photos if you have an Apple TV.

Finally, the last button lets you delete the photo, don't worry about accidently deleting a photo, because it ask you to confirm if you want to delete the photo before you delete it.

Next, let's go to the middle tab. 'Photo Stream' is sort of like 'Flickr'; it lets you share your photos with your family and friends easily. To get 'Photo Stream', tap the 'Shared button on the bottom of the photo app.

Scott La Counte | 111

On the top left corner is a '+' sign; tap it.

This brings up a menu that lets you create a shared directory. From there you can choose the name, who sees it and if it's a public or private photo stream. To choose a person in your contacts tap the blue '+' sign.

Once the album is created, tap the plus sign and tap on each photo you want to add, then hit done.

Once your family or friend accepts your 'Stream' invitation, you will automatically begin syncing your photos. Anytime you add a photo to your album, they will receive a notification.

The new iOS will now also group your photos as memories; it does this by looking at where the photo was taken and when it was taken. So you'll start noticing groups like "Christmas Memories."

Now that you know your way around, it's time to dig into the settings and make this phone completely custom to you!

For most of this chapter, I'll be hanging out in the Settings area, so if you aren't already there, tap Settings from your Home screen.

[7]
ANIMOJI

This chapter will cover:
- This chapter covers:
- What is Animoji
- How To Use Animoji

HOW TO ADD YOUR OWN ANIMOJI

I'm going to be honest, I think Animoji--even creepy! What is it? You almost have to try it to understand it. In a nutshell, Animoji turns you into an emoji. Want to send someone an emoji of a monkey? That's fun. But you know else is fun? Making that monkey have the same expression as you!

When you use Animoji, you put the camera in front of you. If you put out your tongue, the emoji sticks out it's tongue. If you wink, the emoji winks. So it's a way to send a person an emoji with exactly how you are feeling.

To use it, open your iMessage app. Start a text the way you normally would. Tap the App button followed by the Animoji button. Choose an Animoji and tap to see full screen. Look directly into the camera and place your face into the fame. Tab the record button and speak for up to 10 seconds. Tap the preview button to look at the Animoji. Tap the upward arrow button to send or the trashcan to delete.

You can also create an emoji that looks like you. Click that big plus sign next to the other animoji's.

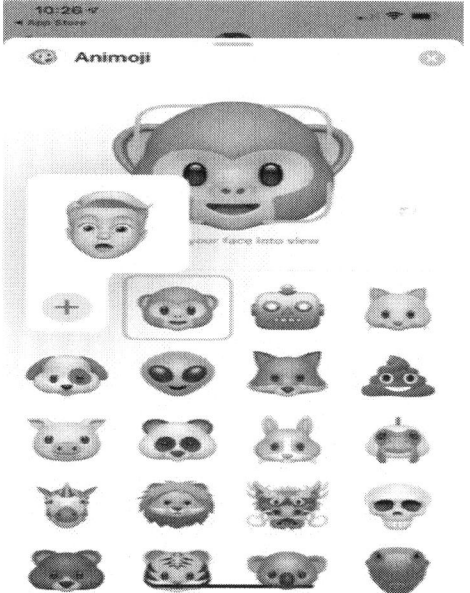

This will walk you through all the steps to send your very own custom animoji--from hair color to type of nose.

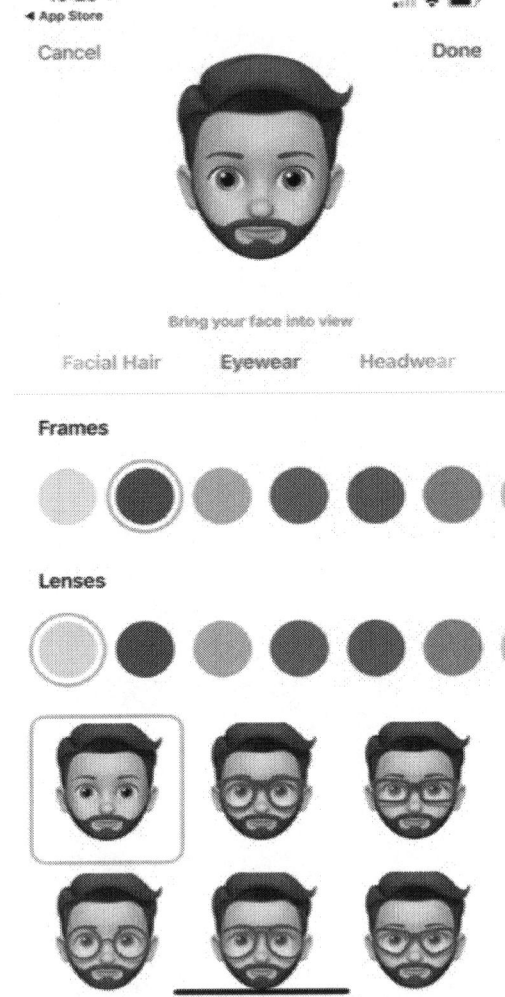

When you're done, you are ready to send.

[8]
HEY, SIRI

This chapter will cover:
- Siri

By now, you probably know all about Siri and how it can remind you of things. If not, press and hold the bottom, square, button on the iPhone to activate it.

So what exactly do you do with it? The first thing you should do is introduce Siri to your family. Siri is pretty smart, and she wants to meet your family. To introduce her to your family, activate Siri by pressing and holding the 'Home' button and say: "Brian is my brother" or "Susan is my boss." Once you confirm the relationship you can now say things like: "Call my brother" or "email my boss."

Siri is also location-based. What does that mean? It means that instead of saying: "Remind me to call wife at 8 am" you can say: "Remind me when I leave work to call wife" and as soon as you step out of the office you will receive a reminder. Siri can be a bit frustrating at first, but it's one of the phone's most powerful apps, so give it a chance!

Everyone hates dealing with waits. There's nothing worse than being hungry and having to wait an hour for a table. Siri does her best to make your life easier by making reservations for you. For this to work, you'll need a free app called 'OpenTable' (you'll also need a free account), which is in the 'Apple App store'. This app makes its money by restaurants paying it, so don't worry about having to pay to use it. Once it's installed, you will simply activate Siri (press the Home button until it turns on) and say: "Siri, make me a reservation at the Olive Garden", (or wherever you want to eat). Note that not all restaurants participate in 'OpenTable', but hundreds (if not thousands) do, and it's growing monthly, so if it's not there, it probably will be soon.

Siri is ever evolving. And with the latest update, Apple has taught her everything she needs to know about sports. Go ahead, try it! Press and hold the 'Home' button to activate Siri, and then say something like: "What's the score in the Kings game" or: "Who leads the league in homeruns?"

Siri has also got a little wiser in movies. You can say: "Movies directed by Peter Jackson" and it will give you a list and let you see a synopsis, the review rating from 'Rotten Tomatoes', and in some cases even a trailer or an option to buy the movie. You can also say: "Movie show times" and a little of nearby movies playing will appear. At this time, you cannot buy tickets to the movie, though one can imagine that option will be coming very soon.

Finally, Siri, can open apps for you. If you want to open an app, simply say: "Open and the apps name."

The new iOS lets you add shortcuts to Siri; you can see this in Settings > Siri & Search > Short cuts.

[9]
MAINTAIN AND PROTECT

This chapter will cover:
- This chapter covers:
- What is Animoji
- How To Use Animoji

SECURITY

Passcode (dos and don'ts, tips, etc.)

In this day and age, it's important to keep your device secure. You may or may not want to set up a touch ID (you will read more about it next), but at the very least it's a good idea to maintain a passcode. Anytime your phone is unlocked, restarted, updated, or erased, it will require a passcode before allowing entry into the phone. To set up a passcode for your iPhone, go to Settings > Passcode, and click on Turn Passcode On. You will be prompted to enter a 4 digit passcode, then re-enter to confirm. Here are a few tips to follow for maximum security:

Do's
DO create a unique passcode that only you would know
DO change it every now and then to keep it unknown
DO select a passcode that can be easily modified later when it's time to change passcodes

Don'ts
DON'T use a simple passcode like 1234 or 5678
DON'T use your birthday or birth year
DON'T use a passcode someone else might have (for example, a shared debit card pin)
DON'T go right down the middle (2580) or sides (1470 or 3690)

ENCRYPTION

With all of the personal and sensitive information that can be stored on iCloud, security is understandably a very real concern. Apple agrees with this, and protects your data with high level 128-bit AES encryption. Keychain, which you will learn about next, uses 256-bit AES encryption - the same level of encryption used by all of the top banks who need high levels of security for their data. According to Apple, the only things not protected with encryption through iCloud is mail (because email clients already provide their own security) and iTunes in the Cloud, since music does not contain any personal information.

KEYCHAIN

Have you logged onto a website for the first time in ages and forgot what kind of password you used? This happens to everyone; some websites require special characters or phrases, while others require small 8 character passwords. iCloud comes with a highly encrypted feature called Keychain that allows you to store passwords and login information in one place. Any of your Apple devices synced with the same iCloud account will be able to load the data from Keychain without any additional steps.

To activate and start using Keychain, simply click on Settings > iCloud and toggle Keychain on, then follow the prompts. After you've added accounts and passwords to Keychain, your Safari browser will automatically fill in fields while you remain logged into iCloud. If you are ready to checkout after doing some online shopping, for example, the credit card information will automatically pre-fill so you don't have to enter any sensitive information at all.

ICLOUD

To really get the full effect of Apple's carefully created ecosystem and be a part of it, you will need to create an iCloud account. Simply put, iCloud is a powerful cloud system that will seamlessly coordinate all of your important devices. The cloud can be a little difficult to understand, but the best way to think about it is like a storage unit that lives in a secure part of the internet. You are allocated a certain amount of space, and you can put the things that mean the most to you here to keep safe. In the case of iCloud, Apple gives you 5 GB for free.

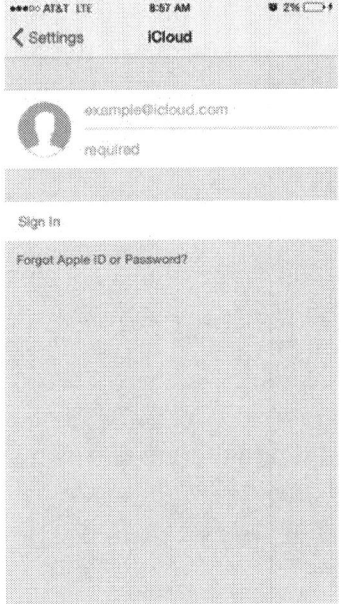

Your phone lets you automatically back up certain files such as your photos, mail, contacts, calendars, reminders, and notes. In the event that your phone is damaged beyond repair or is lost or stolen, your data will still be stored safely on iCloud. To retrieve your information, you can either log onto icloud.com on a Mac or PC, or log into your iCloud account on another iPhone to load the information onto that phone.

With the introduction of iOS 8 and the iPhone 6 and 6 Plus, Apple rolled out a few major changes. You will now be able to store even more types of documents using iCloud Drive and access them from any smartphone, tablet, or computer. Additionally, up to 6 family members will now be able to share purchases from iTunes, iBooks, and the App Store, removing the need to buy an app twice simply because you and a loved one have two different iCloud accounts.

For users who will need more than 5 GB, Apple has dramatically reduced the cost of iCloud:

50 GB is $0.99 per month

200 GB is $2.99 per month
1 TB (1000 GB) is $9.99 per month
2 TB (2000 GB) is $19.99 per month

BATTERY TIPS

The iPhone XS promises better battery life—the longest ever, in fact. But let's face it, no matter how great the battery is, you probably would love to have just a little bit more life in your charge.

Disable Notifications

My mom told me her battery didn't seem to be lasting very long. I looked at her phone and could not believe how many notifications were activated. She knows absolutely nothing about stocks, nor does she have any desire to learn, and yet she had stock tickers going. You might want notifications on something like Facebook, but there are probably dozens of notifications running in the background that you don't even know about, nor do you even need to. Getting rid of them is easy; Go to 'Settings', then to 'Notifications'. Anything that shows up as 'In Notification Center' is currently active on your phone. To disable them, tap on the app and then switch it to off. They aren't gone for good; anytime you want to turn them back on, just go to the very bottom where it says 'Not In Notification Center' and switch them back on.

Brightness

Turning down the brightness just a shade can do wonders for your phone and might even give your eyes some needed relief. It's easy to do; Go to 'Settings', then to 'brightness'. Just move the slider to a 'setting' that you feel comfortable with.

Email

I prefer to know when I get email as soon as it comes. By doing this, my phone is constantly refreshing email to see if anything has come in; this drains the battery, but not too terribly. If you are the kind of person who doesn't really care when they get email, then it might be good to just switch it from automatic to manual. That way it only checks email when you tap the mail button. To switch manual on, go to 'Settings', then to 'Mail, Contacts, Calendars' and finally go to 'Fetch New Data'. Now go to the bottom and tap 'Manually' (you can always switch it back later).

Location, Location, Lo…Battery Hog

Have you heard of location-based apps? These apps use your location to determine where you are exactly. It's actually a great feature if you are using a map of some sort. So let's say you are looking for somewhere to eat and you have an app that recommends restaurants, it uses your GPS to determine your location so it can tell what's nearby. That is great for some apps, but it is not so for others. Anytime you use GPS, it's going to drain your battery, so it's a good idea to see what apps are using it and question if you really want them to. Additionally, you can turn it off completely and switch it on only when needed. To do either, go to 'Settings', then to 'Location Services', switch any app you don't want to use this service to off (you can always switch it back on later).

Accessorize

90% of you will probably be completely content with these fixes and happy with their battery life; but if you still want more, consider buying a batter pack. Battery packs do make your phone a bit more bulky (they slide on and attach to the back of your phone), but they also give you several more hours of life. They cost around $70. Additionally, you can get an external battery charger to slip in your purse or briefcase These packs let you charge any USB device (including iPhones and iPads). External battery chargers cost about the same, the one advantage of a charger versus' a pack is it will charge any device that has a USB, not just the iPhone.

The easiest way to save battery life, however, is to go to Settings > Battery and switch on "Low Power Mode". This is not the ideal setting for normal phone use, but if you only have 20% of your battery and need it to last longer, then it's there.

[10]
MUST-HAVE APPS

> This chapter will cover:
> - Must Have Apps

This list is not going to be full of apps you have heard of. Do you really want me to tell you about a little game called 'Angry Birds'? Or a social networking site called 'Facebook'? If you don't know about the apps, I'm sure someone in your family will tell you all about them as soon as you show them your iPhone. What follows are a few apps you might not know about, but will almost certainly benefit from. Please note that prices are set by the app publishers and may increase or decrease when you look them up.

SignNow: Free

Have you ever received an email with an attachment that needed to be signed? You print it, then scan it, then send it back. SignNow takes away some of those steps;

the app lets you sign a document straight from your phone without the need to print and sign manually.

JotNot: Free. Pro Version: $1.99

Speaking of scanning, 'JotNot' lets you scan a document with your camera. You'll be surprised by the quality of the final document too. It's not the same as scanning, but it's as good as you'll get from a phone.

Google Translate: Free

This app is a travelers' dream. You can speak a word into the translator, and it will tell you how to say it in over two dozen languages. It even pronounces it for you!

SwipeSpeare – Modern Shakespeare: Free

This is a very cool Shakespeare reader. It let's you toggle between the original Shakespeare language and a modern Shakespeare language with the swipe of your finger.

Hipstamatic: Free

You'll quickly discover that there are a lot of camera apps out there. If you are a fan of vintage, then try 'Hipstamatic's app. It will turn your iPhone into a digital antique!

8mm: $1.99

8mm is the same concept as 'Hipstamatic', but instead of taking pictures with old photo cameras, it takes videos with old video cameras.

LoMeIn Ignition: $29.99

Thirty dollars is pretty steep for an app, it's the most you will probably ever pay for an app, so what makes it so great? It can log into your computer remotely from your phone. That means if you are at work and forgot a file on your computer, you can log in and email it to yourself.

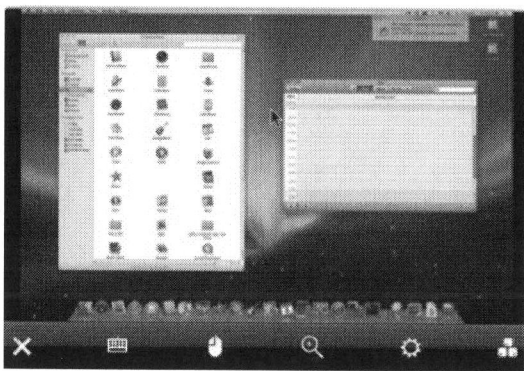

Crackle: Free

If you are a fan of 'Hulu' (the Internet website that lets you stream TV shows and movie for free), but you don't want to pay extra to get 'Hulu+' on your phone, then try 'Crackle'. It has plenty of full-length free shows, and even has free movies.

Flixster: Free

If you go to the movies often, then this is a must have app. It gives you the show times for any movie theater near you using your phone's GPS. Several theaters also let you buy movie tickets directly from the app.

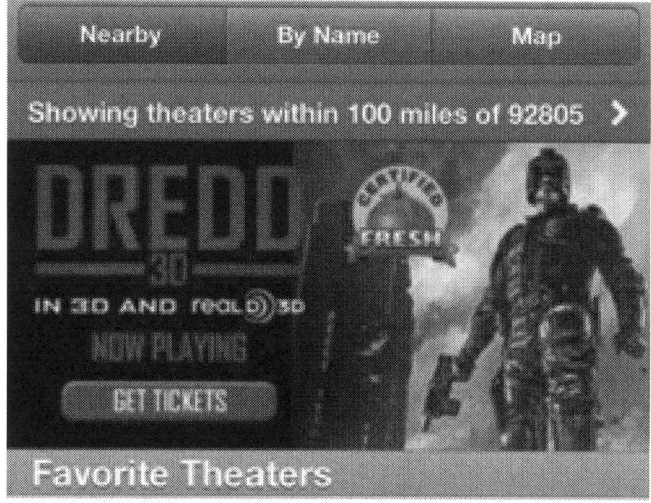

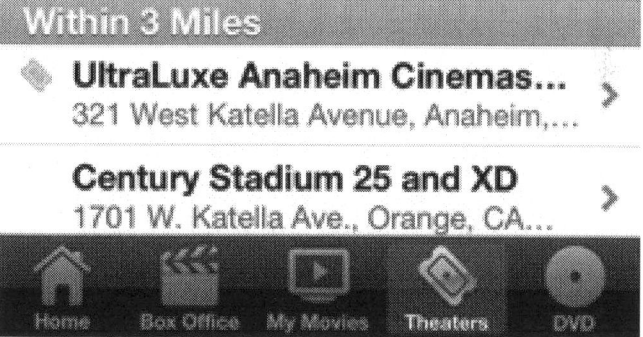

Carcassonne: 9.99

This will probably be the most expensive game you purchase on the iPhone, but it's very much worth it. If you have never played the original strategy board game then you are in for a treat. It's also great if you want to play with others who have an iPhone or an iPad.

132 | *The Ridiculously Simple Guide to iPhone X*

Made in the USA
Columbia, SC
14 February 2022